Learn Hypnosis, Use This Magic To Live A Happy Life, And Help Others Do The Same

AUTHOR NAME

Norman L Bowman C.Ht

DEDICATION

To the people who have given me support and told me that the only way you will ever know if you can do something is to give it your best try, And Trust God to do the rest.

Also Dedicated to my Father Louis (Boots) A. Bowman who was veteran of World War II , And My wonderful Mother Alice Smith. Bowman, And my brother William B. Bowman, Who is still here with me, And without his nagging and staying on my case all the time I guess I would never get anything done.

My Wife Just drove off and left me standing with two Dogs and nothing else, While looking for work I met a guy named Gary Denny
One day I was living in a tent behind a grocery store and the next day I had a whole new family and a job, Thank God for people like Gary Denny and his Family

I would also like to thank my publishers for all they do to make and promote my books and I also want to thank all the people that read them Please keep reading and I promise to be a better writer soon

These people told me you can do anything you set your mind to.

Also to the great people that publish my books, And to the people whose work inspire me to write about the wonders of Hypnosis and Positive Thinking. Now I need inspiration to write A fiction book, So here we go again.

CONTENTS

Norman Bowman C.Ht

ACKNOWLEDGMENTS

Thank You to all the people who put up with me, I know I am a bit grouchy and hard to get along with in general, While I sat and wrote this book and thank you in advance to all the people that will buy this, I hope that it makes positive changes in everyones life that reads the words in this book. Norman

1 CHAPTER

WHAT MAKES IT ALL WORK

Hypnosis is a wonderful art and it helps many people, I would suggest that everyone learn hypnosis because it can enrich your life in so many ways, If you have no desire to be a hypnotist, I would just like to say that the benefits of self hypnosis and meditation are very important to all of us, You have no idea the kind of things you can accomplish through hypnosis, You can completely re-frame your life and overcome most obstacles with hypnosis, I am going to take you on a short journey about what hypnosis is, And what hypnosis can do for you in your life, You can stop smoking, Overcome fears, change just about anything you do not like about yourself, I can go on and on from there. So just read and learn and practice and things you never thought possible will become possible.

What Is Hypnosis:

Well that is a good question and it seems it depend son what a person perceives

it, Because I have seen many contradicting ideas on what it actually is. So I am

going right to the dictionary and see what they say and then we will run threw

what some other seem to think it is.

Definition of *HYPNOSIS from the dictionary – can you believe*

Can You Believe how vague this is and this is out of the dictionary.

1: a trance like state that resembles sleep but is induced by a person whose

suggestions are readily accepted by the subject

2: any of various conditions that resemble sleep

    chapter one text here. Insert chapter one text here. Insert chapter one text here. Insert chapter one text here. Insert chapter one text here. Insert chapter one text here. Insert chapter one text here. Insert chapter one text here. Insert chapter one text here.

Another Example from another dictionary.

Examples of *HYPNOSIS*

He underwent *hypnosis* **to treat his fear of water.**

While **under hypnosis,** she described the horrific accident in detail.

Let me get past the really boring stuff first, I am going to give you a brief rundown of hypnosis is and how it works, And then we will be able to move on to some really cool methods of use that some of these guys have come up with, So bear with me.

About 80% of your mind is subconscious and the other 20% is your conscious mind, The sub conscious mind acts more like a hard drive it takes care of things like body function, Breathing, Heart Beat, Digestion.

Many other functions that we do not have to think about, It just **happens** for us, Thanks to our subconscious mind, That is not all that it does either, It is also a kind of storage locker for the mind as well, And it stores things that we can't really even remember.

It stores many memories that we don't have available without us recalling them, Some can be recalled with no problem but some are so buried in the subconscious that we would have to get professional help to bring them out. If a memory has to much pain involved with it such as something like witnessing a murder or a woman being raped.

Our subconscious mind will basically hide these memories from us for our own protection.

This is because the subconscious mind takes a kind of picture of everything and I mean everything that happens to us all through our lives, For instance I have been in many car and motorcycle accidents in my life and there are parts of those I do not remember that is because my subconscious mind has deemed to painful for me to be able to recall.

Our subconscious also has to prioritize them, The manner that it does this is amazing all by itself, I mean the system that the library has to put books in order has nothing on the human brain, The brain has to take millions of things into consideration when filing memories away, For instance it has to consider how often you will be needing this information, When it stores them away, Because it does not to want to file something that it is always having to get back out all the way at the back of the building if you get my drift,

A memory that has to be recalled on a daily basis is something it would put on the kitchen table so to speak so that it has easy access to it.

The human mind has a wonderful filing system and although it is not driven by emotion and fear and other things like that, It seems to be able to experience compassion about some things, By this I mean like I said before witnessing a murder or a person being raped, These kinds of memories it seems to experience some compassion in the fact that it kind of puts them on the very back shelf as to where your have to put forth effort to bring these memories back.

Another thing you must consider about the subconscious is the enormous amount of information that it has to deal with just on a daily basis much less when you consider that it keeps every memories that ever happens in a persons life, That is awesome to think that it is even possible much less by something the size of the human brain.

Now when you start thinking about all that information, Then you must wonder how it keeps up with it all, Well I do not know, But what I do know is that this is where the conscious mind begins to come into play. It has a great amount of influence on the subconscious mind in this way, It can block information that it deems irrelevant to whatever the situation may be from ever reaching the subconscious mind.

That is why in hypnosis we have to find ways around the conscious mind to get access to the subconscious mind, And that my friends is what keeps hypnotist everywhere coming up with new ways of doing this, One of the best ever in the business of hypnosis was Milton Erickson and he was notorious for coming up with new and exciting ways around the conscious mind, He was way before my time but from what I have read about him he was a bit of a trickster too.

In other words he had a lot of fun learning ways to trick the conscious mind into doing things it would not normally do, He came up with many types of what is called inductions, And sometimes he would have someone in a trance the moment he said hello to them, That is how good he was at what he did and he seemed to have a lot of fun doing it too.

Before I get to far off track let me get back to the fact that the conscious mind makes the decisions about what is important enough to be documented and remembered by the subconscious one reason it is a very necessary thing is you must look at the amount of information that the mind has to hold, As I said before it kind of takes a mental picture of everything that happens to you from the day you are born and files it away.

Just try and imagine how much information this would be, And it is all there, You might have to get a professional to help you recall it but it is all in there somewhere, Can you imagine how over whelming that must be, So there again the conscious mind does a very important job, It kind of sifts through all the information and its relevance to life as it is and then the subconscious minds uses the input from the conscious mind to decide where to file it all.

But if it were not for this wonderful system the information that would be as we say on the tips of or tongues would just be enormous and over whelming in every aspect of the word, When you start to ponder the human mind it will in every way eliminate any doubts about weather we are created by a supreme being or if we just ended up born, lol.

There is an old saying, Where a guy tells another guy well I have forgot more information than you will ever know, Well the truth is as far as I can tell we don;t actually ever forget anything it seems to me it is all just stored away in some kind of remarkable filing system, It is my opinion that we just do not forget anything, We may not be able to recall it, But it is all still in there waiting on the right set of circumstances to bring it all right back to the top of our memories.

The amount of information that we would collect from birth to death would be just a remarkable amount of information that even the fastest and the best computer built to date would never be able to sort it all out.

Alright lets talk for a moment about emotions and what a mess they make of things, Did you know that without emotions getting in the way of our thoughts we could almost succeed at everything we do, Weather you realize it or not our emotions are steady screwing us up in just about every aspect if our lives, Now I am not saying that we would be better off without emotions, Or that the world would be a better place without them I am only stating a fact And that fact is that we would succeed almost 100% of the time if it were not for our emotions getting in the way.

We let so many things from the past influence our future such as bad experiences from our past, Alright lets do a for instance, If we meet a new woman or a new person period, But for now lets stick to the woman thing because I can relate to this very well, We meet this woman and she seems to be everything we ever wanted out of a woman, And our relationship seems to be moving along in a perfect direction, But in the back of our minds even if we are not aware of it, There is a little voice saying something to the effect of you know what happened the last time you loved a woman.

You know what happened the last time you gave into a woman and you let yourself be happy, Every time you get close to someone they just go out and find someone they like better than you and then they just leave you, And you sit around miserable for the next year or so, Or your mind is telling you something to the effect of if she ever gets to know you, You know she won,t be able to love someone like you, Or any other 1000's of combinations of things that your mind can tell you, And after a while you just think well there is know way this is ever going to work out I would save myself some heart ache just to break it off right now.

That is why we need to learn to talk directly to the subconscious mind, once again the subconscious mind just does what it is supposed to do when it is supposed to do it, It is not capable of asking questions about this or that, It just does, It just reacts, This brings to mind the first officer DATA on Star Trek, When they wrote the role for old Data they were on the right track and thats a fact, They had a android that could do anything and everything that a person could do without the emotional hangups of a person.

If we were capable of handling the situations that come up in life without letting our emotions get in the way we could do almost anything, For Instance I have meet a group of people this month that I have never meet before and I have to deliver a sales like talk with them for my business, I am actually almost terrified of public speaking and I will also use hypnosis to get me through it, But if I were just not scared to start with it would be much better wouldn't you say, My conscious mind is allowing fear to interfere with what I must do for the good of my company.

Yes I will be alright and I will do what I have to do and I am sure all will turn out well, But it would be better if I did not have this fear of speaking to start with, So what I must do is use my own self hypnosis mp3's everyday until then to prepare myself for this speaking engagement, So my fear of speaking does interfere with my life any was you look at it.

Another way my fears interfere with my life is about making self hypnosis mp3 to sell, There is a ton of money in selling them on the Internet but I have a southern accent that I am very bothered by and that keeps me from making and marketing mp3's on the Internet, Which probably cuts me out of thousand's of extra dollars in income a year because I have not yet faced the fear of doing them, I hope that now that we are friends you never fall into a trap like this and if you do contact me and I will get you through it, Thats my job and it what I do and I also promise you that I will overcome my own fears too before time to speak at the meeting.

Anyway we need both the conscious and the subconscious mind in every aspect of our life, But we also need to know how to utilize there effect on our lives. I f we were able to take the fear out of our decisions like happens with the subconscious mind does it would make many things we do so much better, But not always action without emotions would not always be a good thing so we need both, What we need more than anything is to be able to call upon each of them at the times we need them and that is what I hope to be able to teach you to do, But it is not simple or easy by any means because it takes a lot of practice to do this.

I am going to do my best to show you how to use both parts of your mind in all the things that you do, But you must want to do this bad, I mean you must want change in your life for the better because it takes commitment and time, Although some of the things I am going to show you in this book can be used right away, Yes I mean you can read it here and now and walk right out the door and start using it on everyone you meet and I really feel that you will experience positive change right away, That is how powerful some of these methods are.

And the simplicity of some of them is also wonderful, Some of the things I am going to teach you are going to be so simple you are not going to believe that they will work but I promise you if you use the methods that I teach you will see positive results almost right away, We will get to teaching the how to do a little bit later in the book, Right now the how and why it all works is the important thing now.

If you do not have any idea how something works then you will never be able to make up your own Inductions, Pre Talks and other things that you will need to be able to do once you understand how it all works, Most everything that you learn from would be useless to you without knowing why they work so lets go ahead and spend the necessary time learning why they work, So once you have learned it all you will not need to be a slave to someone else's ideas, And another thing about knowing all of this extra information is that you will be able to do things for your clients that others cannot do.

When you look at a picture of a brain you see one big piece and not a very attractive piece ether it is in my opinion kind of ugly but I really don't think weather or not I think it is pretty has much to do with this conversation, Your brain is actually two complete separate parts, When we talk about the conscious and the subconscious we are really talking about two complete separate things that word independent of each other, There are thousands of different ways to explain all about this and I am no different I have my way of explaining and I do it this way because of the simplicity of it, Your brain is made up of the conscious and subconscious the conscious mind is only about 20% of the whole brain and the subconscious makes up the other 80%, Now let me say that my this what most people figure is close to the way they are divided I have no idea if anyone knows exactly.

But we talked a lot about this earlier the conscious mind is the emotional part of the mind it makes all of your decisions and it is also able toy mix decision making with emotions, For instance if you see a homeless person asking for change on the side of the road and you dig into your pocket and find that all you have is what you put in there to get yourself a cup of coffee on your way to where you are going, you dig in there and give it to him anyway thinking he may need a cup of coffee worse than you do.

You let your emotions get between you and a nice hot cup of coffee, Well chances are if you subconscious mind was responsible for this decision you may have very well got your nice warm cup of coffee and the homeless man may have had to do without, Because you let your emotions guide your decision, Your subconscious mind would not have let this happen, Your subconscious mind would have done exactly what you had intended to do when you put the change in your pocket and it would not have been swayed by anything.

That part of your brain is not capable of feeling the emotions that led you to give away that change. That is why being able to use your both parts of your mind can be a wonderful thing, In every part of life, But the problem is if everyone made decisions based on the way your subconscious mind would do it it might just be a very cold world to live in, However if you can balance the difference and use the each individual parts of your mind to do what they are good at then a whole new world of possibilities will open up for you and that is what we are going to attempt to do.

We must learn how to use the subconscious mind to do our bidding without giving it enough rope to become a heartless monster that it could be if we let it. We are going to learn how to do this in this book we are going to learn how to use our subconscious mind to do our bidding without allowing it to turn us into a heartless machine, Our goal Is to learn to get by the conscious mind and be able to speak directly to the subconscious mind, There are tons of ways to do this, You can trick your way past it you can shock your way past it, Or you can just develop the skill to know when it is sitting there wide open and waiting for you.

Once you learn to speck directly to the sub conscious mind you have everything you need to be able to solve problems for yourself and others, Unfortunately I have found that it is much easier to talk to another persons mind than it is to speak to your own mind, Habits die very hard and I am a testament to that, I have been trying to Stop Smoking forever it seems but the one things lacking from my efforts to quit is the fact that I deep down in my heart just don't really want to stop.

Some of the things that are coming up in this book have already been gone over, No you are not going crazy It is just that somethings need to be said a few times for you to get the full grasp and meaning of everything I am saying so be patient and I promise I will get you where you are going and I will get you there on time to.

Hypnosis works almost completely with the Subconscious mind when properly used, It bypasses the conscious mind and allows a skilled person to speak right to our subconscious mind, There are many ways of doing this, And that is what I hope to teach you to do in this book, But first I need to explain this so that you will know more about how and why this works, The subconscious mind is not a thinker, It is a doer, When it sets out to do things it lets nothing get in its way.

For instance, The conscious mind might allow fear to keep it from doing a certain things, Not the subconscious, when it has something to do, It has no emotion, fear, Or otherwise else that would influence the conscious mind.

So when a suggestion hit's the spot and by the spot I mean the subconscious mind, The subconscious sets out to do what it has been told to do, Without fear or concern for anything else, That is also why a hypnotist must be very cautious about how he words the suggestion he gives the subconscious mind.

Let me give you an example, When you are hypnotizing someone to stop smoking a lot of hypnotist will say when you think about a cigarette you will get a bad taste in your mouth and you will get a funny smell in your nose until the urge passes, Now someone not thinking may say when you think about a cigarette you will get sick at your stomach until the urge passes, You Never Want To Do This, Because when the person thinks about a cigarette they are very subject to start throwing up all over the place, (YES) it will make them physically Ill, Again You Never Want To Do This your client will get physically Ill.

Now that is just one example of a screw up you can make by not thinking, You must think everything out before you put a suggestion into the subconscious mind because it takes you quite literally and does exactly what you told it to do, And you will never have any repeat clients, Like that and you may well get sued also, So THINK about what you are doing, I am going to try to give you a proper suggestion for Stop Smoking Hypnosis but even then, Double Check, I do, I have to, I make mistakes, And you cannot do that when you are responsible for what is going on in a persons mind.

A better way to do a stop smoking suggestion would be to say something like – When you get an urge for a cigarette you will immediately realize (That you are a non smoker and cigarettes taste terrible to you) Now I will be teaching you some hypnosis scripts later, There will be a complete stop smoking script for you to use if you wish.

You must always think about what you say when talking to someones subconscious mind, Because somethings you put in there by accident could lead to a Injury or a Illness, So you are playing with some very serious stuff here, And yes, I do make jokes about hypnosis and Nlp but you must realize that it can be a very dangerous thing in the wrong hands, So you must strive to think everything out before you do it, It is very important to your future as a hypnotist and having friends because if you mess up with some people they get mad and stay mad, Lets move on with.

We have determined that the subconscious mind acts without

emotion of any kind and that is what makes it such a valuable asset to you, A skilled hypnotist can help you do just about anything with your subconscious, I have once again went way to far with this explanation I am sure you understand what hypnosis is now and I can begin teaching you how to do it. There are some things in this book that I am sure I am spending to much time on and there are some that I am repeating a few times but the thing is if you are going to learn how to do something and you want to do it well you just have to go through it many times, So as I tell my Dog when I am teaching her a new trick here we go again.

2 CHAPTER

Some Different Methods

I am going to try to explain to the best of my ability how hypnosis works, And I am going to use people in here that I kind of look up to in this trade, But I want to remind you that are should goal here is not just to get to be a hypnotist are a great showman, Our goal is to learn how to live a happy life and to be a asset to others, The only thing on this earth that will ever make you happy is when you have a feeling of accomplishment and one of the best ways to do that is by way of helping others and being a asset to life itself.

You can not buy or borrow happiness nor can your get you get it by having wonderful things that everyone is jealous of, The only way to live a happy life is to earn it by your actions, And I will spend some time later showing you some ways to get started doing just that, There are exercises and mind games I like to call them that will help you achieve real happiness, Read into what I am writing and more so when I start writing about self hypnosis but remember all hypnosis techniques will work as self hypnosis, That hard head we are trying to break here may just be your own.

Hypnosis is a real and normal state of mind, As a matter of fact we drift in and out of hypnosis all during the day when we are doing what we consider ordinary tasks, such as driving, Watching TV, And on and on. Hypnosis is a state of mind between asleep and awake and I am going to show you how to achieve this with yourself and anyone else you wish to achieve it with.

I pray that I have given you a at least round about idea of what we have to do to reach the state of hypnosis in someone, However I do feel as if I have wasted a tone of time beating around the bush but I see no reason to teach you something without giving you all the reasons I can for how it all works, But simply put you just must bypass the logical mind or the conscious mind to reach the subconscious mind. And it seems to me that I have at least explained that the conscious mind is emotional and the sub-conscious is not emotional and that makes all the difference in the world.

After wasting a ton of time on this I just bet everyone will have a different idea about what I have said, So I am going to go out on a limb here and say that it can be a state of mind brought on also by hum drum activities,

This is when so called Covert Hypnosis and Street Hypnotist can come into play, People that practice this type of hypnosis count a great deal on this state of mind, This is also handy for you to know when you are wanting to plant a suggestion about a certain thing in someones mind, Soon I am going to get into Nlp and some Covert hypnosis and you will learn very fast that this is a good time to prey on a person, When they are suffering from mid afternoon sleepiness or just plain boredom, This is a wonderful time to plant suggestions and they will for the most part not even notice.

When a street hypnotist or common thief that uses hypnosis to steal, They count on this state of mind to catch you off guard, But lets stick to what a street hypnotist would do, When they go to pick someone off the street to hypnotize.

See, most all of us are already in a trance while going threw everyday task, Because our minds are not challenged by the activity we are doing at that moment, We simply let our minds remove us from where we are at that particular moment in time and place us a trance state, I feel our minds are saying there is somewhere I would rather be, It is even possible that we are in a state of mental rest, Now this is my opinion and I am hardly an expert on the human mind, But what I do know is that hypnotist also counts on this to get us into the trance like state, They need us in this trance like mental state where they can easily place there suggestions in our minds.

Street hypnotist count on the fact when they walk up on someone on the street that they are already in a trance like state, That is why they can simply walk up to someone and just distract them and ask for there wallet and a person just gives it to them, Not quite that simple but you will learn how they do it in this book, I will show you how they do what they do, But you must have the common sense not to run out and start doing it you will go to jail.

Basically the hypnotist distracts them and confuses them, And the hypnotist moves on quickly and it takes the person a few seconds to realize what has happened, Hypnosis is sometimes a state of mind that we go to unknowingly when we are just bored, Just walking perhaps is one of the most boring things we can do when we see the same old things day after day it is know fun anymore, So we just drift off into our own little world, And in this state is when we are most subject to be taken advantage of by a hypnotist that knows this.

I have been fascinated by a Hypnotist slash Magician named Derren Brown, He does some things which are just outrageous and I know by watching him he takes advantage of this state of mind in most everything he does, I am not going into a lot of the things he does because I do not want to give you any ideas that will wind you up in jail, But I am going to tell you how he pulls off some of his stunts, And you should be able to see yourself in the people he does these things to.

What I mean is that you will recognize the states of mind and you will no that you have been in them from time to time, And to benefit you by knowing how to spot this frame of mind in people, And how to use it to your advantage, One thing I have seen him do is go into a subway and ask everyone where they are going to get off and he seems to make them just forget, And some of them get really mad to when they miss there stop.

Well what better place than a subway to find bored people, People who are in the mind frame we were discussing, Well there is no better place and I am not sure how he does what he does but you can do the same thing, He does it by catching the person kind of off guard and first asking him if he ever had anything on the tip of your tongue and just forgot, And then he proceeds to ask them a question and with a snap of his finger they will forget until he snaps them out of the confusion, Now this takes a but of practice but it almost always works.

There are tons of ways you can put suggestions out there and people will just react, With out rhyme or reason to it, They just react and that is something that anyone can do with practice, You can learn to use it to your advantage in many situations, People are predictable and they are also creatures of habit and the more you know this, The more things you will begin to see from a whole new perspective, The power of hypnosis is a very powerful thing, And some say it is just a placebo as a matter of fact, I say it is just a placebo, But it is like everything else in life, If you believe it, It is true and that my friends is a fact.

Your mind actually does all the work, It just needs the power of intense suggestion to go to work, The mind is a wonderful and powerful thing.

But if you look at it like hypnosis is a tool used to put your mind to work, Then it turns from a placebo to a real working thing again, And yes I do know I am kinda going around in circles, But the good news is I am doing it to make a point. So when we get through the next few Chapters you can make up your own mind is it placebo or medicine, Whatever it is, It is a powerful thing.

People have and I am sure still do go through surgeries with no more than hypnosis for anesthesia, Amazing right, And who do I think I am to call this miracle a placebo, Well you be the judge when you are done with this book you e-mail me and tell me what you think, Because I am going to bring out the evidence and you decide, Weather it is a placebo or not, The world is a better place with hypnosis.

Hypnosis is as real as anything a Psychologist can do for you, Because his main job is to get your mind on the right track, Well hypnosis does this also, But the work is done by your mind, I am gonna go back to NLP for just a few moments, You can actually walk up to someone you do not know on the streets, They can be smoking a cigarette at the time you do this, You say something like (You Don't Smoke) to them. And they will probably look at you like you are nuts and go on about there business, Cool, But what (has) happened is that what you said bypassed the conscious mind altogether, But not the Subconscious mind, And weather or not they heard it.

Your Sub Conscious mind will act on it, In some way not have the pleasure to them they used to have, And they will be on the road to quitting, Also it will make it easier to quit when they figure it out, This will not happen 100% of the time, But if it only happens to say 1 out of 10 of the people you said it to, It would be great for them.

Nlp is a great tool also and it does work just as hypnosis does, And in some cases it is much easier to use that hypnosis, Nlp can be used anywhere anytime for just about any reason, Now when you use Nlp you must say what you say with authority, Like you own them, You do not say well maybe you do not smoke you must say it with authority, (You Do Not Smoke) and whoever you said it to will be on there way to stopping, There are millions of ways Nlp and Hypnosis can be used and I will never be able to cover them all but I will cover enough to give you a clear understanding of them both and you will be able to go out and take a quick certification class and you will be on the way to practicing hypnosis for a living.

A good hypnotist can go right to the subconscious mind in a matter of minutes, Actually I can do this in second but it is not always appropriate for everyone for instance, People have an idea about hypnosis and how it works from TV and books (Fictions) and that is what they expect, And you will find when you are dealing with the mind you have to go with what is expected because in the short run that will work better for you, By having an idea what is going to happen in a hypnotist office these people are what we called conditioned already.

They were conditioned by TV shows books however they got the idea it does not matter, Where ever they got the idea that place or person has done part of your work for you by making them think it is going to be a certain way.

By them already having a idea of how it works they have already conditioned there mind to believe that they can be hypnotized a certain way, Therefore all you have to do is follow the template they have laid it all out for you and give them what they expect and they will drift right into a trance, EASY MONEY I like to say, Many times we have to spend about 45 minutes to get a person ready for the induction, But by them coming in with a particular idea of what it going to take to get them into a trance all you have to do is.

We are going to dance around here for a few more minutes before moving on, Lets go back to Derren Brown for a few minutes not only because he is my hero but because, I can tell you what he has done and then how he did it and it will give you a clearer understanding of how Nlp and Hypnosis works, He does a bit where he goes up to a perfect stranger on the street and ask directions to somewhere and then throws in another quick question about that place.

Then he reaches out to shake hands with the guy and when the guy goes to shake his hand he pulls it back and looks away, Then after this he says while you are at it, Just give me your watch, Your Wallet, And your house keys, And then he walks off right away, The guy knows something happened but he is not sure what he just stands there for a minute and when he realizes what he has done he goes after Derren.

Now what has happened that allowed Derren to do this to him, Derren asked him for directions, While the guy is still trying to tell him the directions he asked another question about what was in the building, And while all of this was going on Derren held out his hand towards the guys water bottle and the guy gave it to him.

While the poor guy was still giving directions Derren reached toward the guys water bottle and the guy gave it to him not thinking, While the rest of this was going on Derren reached out to shake his hand and withdrew it before the guy could make contact to shake his hand, Derren gives back the water bottle.

Then Derren asked him first watch, wallet, and house keys, And the guy was steading giving them to him, How did Derren do this,

Well it was a combination of many things Derren did quickly.

He asked this guy directions, While the guy was trying to give the answer to the first question Derren asked another creating more confusion, Just after he asked the second question Derren took the water bottle from him or he really just reached out to it and the guy handed it to him, Why because he was thinking about something else, As Derren gave back the water bottle he is also reaching out to shake his and when the guy goes to shake his hand he withdraws it.

Then Derren asked for his watch and while the guy is taking off his watch he says why not give me your wallet too, And he asked for his house keys and the guy is steady giving, Why was Derren able to do this, Why did this guy go along with it, How did Derren pull it off, Well it was not one thing Derren did it was everything Derren did.

I will explain as best I can and I am not sure I saw everything he did either but here goes, The first thing is he did it very quickly, First question, Second question, Water bottle, Hand shake, Look away, ask for watch, wallet and house keys, How did he do it well let us first go back to something I think I said earlier we are all in a state of trance when we are walking on a route we often take.

It is mostly because we are somewhat bored, We see the same scenery day in and day out so we get bored with it, Derren pops up and asked him directions, This is something new to be asked for directions, So he broke his pattern when he asked him for directions, Before the guy could recover from that he asked him another question, Confusing him even more.

Derren held his hand out for the water bottle without thinking the guy gave it to him, Derren gives it back planting the suggestion he can be trusted among other things going on here, Derren reaches for his hand to shake it pulling it back and looking away creating more confusion, Man is pretty much lost right now and Derren asked him for his watch the guy is still trying to give directions from the first question, Derren asked for his watch, Guy is taking it off and handing it to him.

Derren says while we are at it lets have the wallet and house keys also, Guy does what he is asked to do, Derren walks off smiling,

The guy is standing there trying to understand what just happened Derren stops and waits for him to figure it out and give him his things back.

I am not sure I can explain all of what Derren did because it happens fast but I can tell you this he did it with confusion and speed, Also before I go further Derren also uses a lot of hand movements and pointing in the opposite direction and such to add to the confusion, Alright he interrupted the guys pattern when he asked him for directions before the guy can answer the first question Derren asks another adding to the confusion, Derren reached out for the guys water bottle,

(The water bottle is more than just a bottle to Derren he is testing the water and the amount of confusion he has caused this guy) the guy gave water bottle Derren gives back water bottle (Plants Suggestion He Can Be Trusted) Derren is pointing in several directions adding to the confusion, Derren asked for watch adding to the confusion, Derren asked for wallet adding to confusion, Derren asked for house keys adding to confusion, And finally Derren walks off adding to the confusion.

It takes guy about 45 to 60 seconds to realize what he has done, Man looks around for Derren still in somewhat of a daze, Man sees Derren up the block and slowly moves his way to ask for his stuff back.

I have no idea if I did a good enough job of painting this picture or explaining how he did it to make sense, But Derren is one of the greats in the field and I am telling you at this point go to YOUTUBE and type in his name and watch some of his videos and learn from a master.

I am going to try and explain a little better and then we will move on to another, First Derren knew when he stopped him and asked directions he would interrupt the guys pattern, By that I mean he was already somewhat confused, Derren starts asking questions, Quick, The hand gesture he is asking for directions to a place that is in one direction and pointing the other direction, adding to the guysconfusion, Derren then just reaches toward the water bottle I do not know what was in Derrens mind but I have to think he was testing the guy to see how suggestible he was, And how confused he was Derren is a master at this, I am going to run one or two more across you so you get a clear understanding of what I think he is doing from a professional stand point, Bear in mind I am not in this guys caliber so bear with me.

Let me watch another vis real quick so I can give you fresh information, I want to be the one to admit that many things Derren Brown does are way over my head as I said before he is the best as far as I am concerned, But we are going to try and find a simple one that I can explain and you can get some value out of.

There is one more video that Derren Brown does where he uses self hypnosis on his self to become a wax statue and he has a Nlp tape running on the intercom using a classic Nlp or Hypnosis suggestions to freeze everyone in the wax museum, We will go through this whole deal later and I will explain how he does it in length, Now you are wondering can I teach you to do some of the things he does, Well yes I can all in good time, We have a lot of ground to cover first though I am afraid.

3 CHAPTER

STUFF YOU CAN DO NOW

Some other tricks you can start doing right away, Well not a trick it is Nlp, But I warn you now you better practice these things in front of a mirror first or you will wind up getting laughed at, Before you get it to work on anyone, You can use sentences such as (You Like Me) don't like sitting around all the time do you, I was watching a movie the other night and those people on that movie were (excellent lovers) , That fellow over there looks like a very (hard working man), I saw a new guy on the news he seemed very (trustworthy) in his approach to news.

The important part of these sentences is the parts I put into parenthesis this is what you want to link yourself to, How do you do that it is very easy, All you have to do when you say the sentence softly pat your chest or the table, No I do not mean like Tarzan tapped his chest just softly pat your chest or tap the table when you say that exact part of the sentence, Like this, You like me (Pat as you are saying you LIKE ME) don't like sitting around all day.

Do this on the key words that you want attached to you, Anything, Even best lover, Now you may or may not get a immediate response but once the sub conscious mind interprets what you have said even if it is hours later, From then on when that person thinks of you they will attach these words to your memory, That is a fact, I think I mentioned before about the smoking thing, That you could tell a person that is smoking a cigarette that they are a non smoker and they may think you are nuts when you say it but eventually there sub conscious will start acting on that and they will enjoy smoking less and less until they just quit.

No this does not work every last time but it works much more than it fails that is a promise.

So where we are now is that you can sit at home at night and figure ways to get your Anchors into sentences and practice saying them without looking crazy and once you perfect this you are on your way to changing just about anything you want to about your life, When you start to get really good at this you can use it on job interviews or anything else you want to use it on, And sometimes it will have an immediate response and sometimes it will take a bit to sink in.

But the fact is even if it is days later when that person thinks about you he will also think about the anchor you put with your memory, Now moving on to some other things you can do with this type of Nlp.

Now hoping that I have made my point so far lets see where we can go from here, Another way you can use Nlp without being to obvious is to use it to help your friends in simple ways, Like when you see a guy or girl friend first thing in the morning you can say something to the effect of (you are having a wonderful day today), (You really feel good today) , (You are happy today) , Now I know it is hard to fit saying things like this in just anywhere but with a little practice you can do it and I know your friends mean a lot to you so they are worth it.

Here is a way to do it that will not look quit as strange, (You Feel Great Today) Right, And leave it like a question but use the anchoring technique and do the table tap or the glass tap to set the anchor and you have done it without looking Daft, There are many ways to do these anchors and I will help you more a little deeperinto the book but right now I am trying to cover a lot of territory, And this is (A Great Book) and you are having a (lot of fun reading it) .

Many times painting a picture for your subjects is just what you have to do, When you paint the picture for them say all things as though they have already happened, That you know what you are saying to be fact, There is no room for doubt in hypnosis, There is no room for a lack of confidence in hypnosis either.

What you need to do right this minute if you have a confidence problem is go to a search engine and type in FREE Hypnosis mp3's for confidence, Go and download the best one you can find for free and start using it just before you go to sleep every night for at least a month, If you can make time use it twice a day, There are some good free vid's out there and they do work you will begin to feel the change in about two days of using it.

The most important things about hypnosis and Nlp is confidence and delivery of the anchor or suggestions you are using, I am going to do a flip flop and talk about hypnosis for a bit now, Hypnosis is just a little different from Nlp, Hypnosis needs a trance like state most of the time, Not always But most of the time, There are about a million ways to induce a trance, Here is my favorite but it is notgood for every situation, And that would be the rapid induction, The hand shake, The arm pull, Hand drop rapid induction, Palm magnets to hand clasp shock.

Induction, Direct gaze shock induction, Some of these induction are much easier than others that is something that works for some better than others kind of thing, You must practice them and see what works best for you.

Instant inductions can be done to anyone, anywhere, but you need to take care when doing instant induction hypnosis. Rapid inductions can be fun, but make sure when you are hypnotizing someone that they have consented to be hypnotized.

Otherwise the outcome of the instant induction might be an instantly angry person. Instant hypnosis can be distressing if it is unexpected hypnosis.

Rapid inductions are very powerful, be sure that you are ready to handle the result before you try them, We are going to spend a good bit of time on safety and ethics very soon now.

Long inductions are what you will find you be using the most they are not the easiest but unfortunately when you are charging what I charge I do not mind going the long road and it is what most people are going to expect thanks to TV and books that have people getting hypnotized in them, A long induction consist of several parts, The pre talk as a rule I spend about anywhere from 15 minutes to 45 minutes on this, Whatever it takes to ensure I have smooth sailing when I am ready to trance a person.

Also bear in mind the pre talk is like the setup for the whole deal and if you blow the pre talk you may have blown the whole hypnosis session, I as a rule ask a bunch of questions Health is the first thing you should be asking about because some people should not go under hypnosis, I stay away from anyone who has seizures, anyone who has any possibilities of a brain tumor and there is a whole bunch of stuff you need to watch out for.

Once again I am going to pass you off to another book or lessons, I have a book that goes into this stuff very deeply if you are planning to do this for a living you need to read the (Get Certified Book Of Mine) or you can take your lessons from someone else if you like, But you need all the information if you are going to start doing hypnosis for a living, Now the other questions I am very interested in are things like what where do they like to go on vacation and yes there is a reason for it.

And what kind of music they like, These things after you get pass the health questions are all information for me, I find when someone ids in my office if I can set a scene or atmosphere to make a person more comfortable the quicker I can get them into a trance state.

You must remember that a trance is really nothing more than a deep sate of relaxation therefore anything I can do to induce relaxation the better it works for me, There are other hypnosis that I know do things other ways but the ways I am telling you about work great for me so, I suggest you do a lot of reading on the subject of hypnosis and don't put all your apples in one cart as they say, These methods work for me but I am never to old or to good at what I do to listen to someone whit more experience on a matter and I suggest you be the same way, Since you are dealing with other peoples well being when it comes to hypnosis.

Once you get passed the pre talk, You are ready for the induction, If you are in an office situation I suggest music that your client like or sound effects they like, Such as sounds of the ocean or rain falling, Or soft meditation music or elevator music playing softly in the back ground.

Also I suggest you practice a lot before you try to induce trance in this way and remember what you are supposed to say and when you are supposed to say it, So you make as few mistakes as possible after you have done this for awhile and are no longer nervous about it you will find you can pretty much cover up any mistake you might make but you can never get enough practice, I cannot tell you what to use I can tell you that the eye fixation works best for me in an office situation.

Have them pick out a spot on the wall and tell them to pick a spot where they have to look up a little bit, You do not want them to have to move there whole head up to see the spot you just want them to have to have there eyes looking up a tad, This brings on eye fatigue a little quicker than if they were looking straight in front of them, Tell them to make sure there feet are flat on the floor.

And let there hands rest in there lap or on there legs or on the arm of the chair there comfort is very important at this point, Soften your voice to your hypnosis voice very soft but yet firm, Have them take several deep breaths, Have them inhale threw there nose and out through there mouth, Have them take deep slow breathes tell them when they take these breaths they should feel it in the belly,After they have taken the second breath tell them they are doing good, At this point I am going to give you the words to a pre written script to work with and to practice with at home NOW if you are planning on doing this. Rapport is everything from this point on remember **confidence.**

I am ready to give you your first induction so that you can start to practice it, But I am going to give you a little more of an explanation of why we are doing some things first because again the more you understand the better you will be at this, Also I know I am just a little bit on the crazy side but I really do care if you succeed at this or not, If you are my student I want you to do well and be an example of my work and when you tell someone you learned from me I will take a lot of pride in that so here goes with a tad more information on the whys of things we do, Here gaining rapport of the person whom you want to hypnotize is what is most essential when you want to learn how to hypnotize, This was also why I said I spend up to 45 minutes on my pre-talks some times is to build the strongest rapport possible before I begin to hypnosis process.

This is a phenomenon of letting the other person feel that he or she shares the same wavelength as yours. This is a state of sync where you can even match to the persons breathing rhythm. This is a harmonious relation that is expressed and your subject will tend to listen to your suggestions and perform accordingly, Alright are you ready let us proceed. Speak slow and soft and firmly, Start just like this.

(Remember eyes up if possible to bring on eye fatigue faster),From where you are sitting comfortably, you can just pick a spot on the wall in front of you... perhaps the top corner of the picture, or that spot on the wall there where the reflection is creating a small rainbow.

Great. Now, let your eyes rest on that .... and just look at that point.... just keep focusing on that spot, without moving your eyes...

(Take time for your breathing to match theirs)

And while you keep looking at that spot, wondering around it but coming back to it with your eyes in a gentle easy going comfortable way, you can become aware of the muscles around your eyes.... how they they are holding your eyes up....

that's right... and your eyelids... and what they feel like....

You may [wait for them to blink] blink a bit more frequently [wait for them to blink again] that's right... and your breathing might get deeper, as you relax.

Now, as your eyes are resting on that spot on the wall,

attracting your focus, your mind wrapped around the idea of that spot on the wall where your eyes are resting now,

the eyelids may perhaps become heavy... or your eyes want to close.

But I don't want you to close them just yet.

Let them remain open.

And blinking [wait for them to blink] that's it, even more frequently now. You

might wonder if that blink is slower than normal....

And lots of people, as they begin to enter trance, find that their focus becomes

increasingly fuzzy... vision getting dim and misty... And as you look at that spot

you might see that it begins to waver... or maybe you see it blurring ... or that

spot changes shape or color...

[Pause]

That's it...

You may have noticed your arms and legs are getting heavy, as your eyelids get

heavier and heavier. And as you think about how nice it would be to allow your

eyes and eyelids to relax... and close those tired eyes...

As you focus your eyes on that spot and as they become more tired and more heavy and

more fatigued...

When you are ready, you can close your eyes. [Their eyes may already be closed

by now. If so, you would go straight onto the next line.]

[Pause]

And closing those eyes means you can relax now.... It feels so good... so

peaceful... as you really let yourself relax...

Breathing in for just a moment and breathing out, allow the relaxation to double

again throughout your entire body. Going deeper and deeper into a wonderful

state of relaxation.

deeper... deeply, that's it... all the way...all the way...

[Pause]

(Proceed to Deepener) We will do deepeners later:

Alright you have completed a whole trance once you can do this we will move on to deepeners and more but now just work on this and continue reading and

PRACTICE, PRACTICE, PRACTICE I am going to go into some other ways to hypnotize and we will get to deepeners a little later, There are so many different ways to hypnotize people that I want to give you some fun things you can do with a practice partner such as sum quick inductions.

You can have a lot of fun with these at parties and just for fun about anywhere you are at but be careful and check local laws about hypnosis because it is Illegal in a few places. I feel it is time to teach you some fast inductions that can be fun at parties and other places and I know for a fact they will be a blast for you because it always is the first time you are able to trance someone, A good hypnotist can go right to the subconscious mind in a matter of minutes, Actually I can do this in second but it is not always appropriate for everyone for instance.

People have an idea about hypnosis and how it works from TV and books (Fictions) and that is what they expect, And you will find when you are dealing with the mind you have to go with what is expected because in the short run that will work better for you, By having an idea what is going to happen in a hypnotist office these people are what we called conditioned already, They were conditioned by TV shows books however they got the idea it does not matter, Where ever they got the idea that place or person has done part of your work for you by making them think it is going to be a certain way.

By them already having a idea of how it works they have already conditioned there mind to believe that they can be hypnotized a certain way, Therefore all you have to do is follow the template they have laid out for you and give them what they expect and they will drift right into a trance, EASY MONEY I like to say, Many times we have to spend about 45 minutes to get a person ready for the induction.

But by them coming in with a particular idea of what it going to take to get them into a trance all you have to do is, I would like to give everyone that reads this book a all round look at hypnosis from all directions, Hypnosis is not a fragile thing and it can be done in many ways.

To hypnotize all you must do is interrupt the thought pattern for a split second and even though this not always get you to the point where the person goes into a deep trance the suggestions you make during this moment of time do impact that person weather they feel hypnotized or not, As a matter of fact you can plant deep and long lasting suggestions that a person will act on weather they realize it or not in this moment of time, That is not good for show though and it is also not good to have someone leave your office that thinks you have done nothing, So it is always good to achieve a trance like state, But what I am saying is a trance is not necessary to get the desired result from the person.

4 CHAPTER

More Trances For Your

Many people will not go into a trance for many reasons and one of those is simply not believing in hypnosis, You van help that person though despite there self, But will that pay your bills, No it will not, You must achieve trance in most situations but you do not need a trance to help a person, Say you have a friend who smokes and you feel his life would be better not smoking.

You can absolutely help this person without them even knowing you have helped them, But this kind of hypnosis will not pay your bills but it may well help you sleep better at night, I have already been through many ways to this this so if you do not remember read back it is there, As far as making a living with hypnosis trance is needed so if you run across someone who has a strong belief they can not be hypnotized just move on to someone who wants to be hypnotized, Everyone can be hypnotized but is it fruit full for you to take the time just to prove this to them, No it is not, It is a waste of your time so move along.

I have little patients for those who are to hard headed for there own good but sometimes such as with family we must help them despite there hard heads, I have also already covered ways to do this so just be p resistant with them and you will win, I have stop smoking groups and weight lose groups because I do not believe in just doing hypnosis on a person and saying go home, Don't eat so much and you won't be fat or go home I have done all I can if you do not quit smoking after our hypnosis session well there must be something wrong with you, No No No when you take a persons money for a service you must to best of your ability do what you said you were going to do, And if after our very best efforts you cannot help them, Well so people do fall through the cracks.

Do not set up a practice just because you can, Or based on greed, If you do not like helping people and you are a hypnotist, Be a show hypnotist, Do not hang out a sign that says you help people lose weight or quit smoking unless you are willing to do what it takes to help them, So I have group follow ups, My time is very very valuable and I am not going to waste it, And your time is never wasted when you are helping someone, I do weight lose and stop smoking hypnosis in there office visits for $300.00 That is one 90 minute visit and two 45 minute visits and then free group follow ups, So they can go to group sessions until they can handle there problem on there on.

Do not take someones money unless you are willing to go all the way with them, Karma will get you my friends, That is a fact and if I thought the kind of people who would do this were reading this book I would delete right this second, By writing this book I am helping people maybe find there place in life helping others, If you are not a person of moral value I do not want to help you, Fact.

Lets move on to bypassing the conscious mind by trickery I suppose, Have you ever have someone not finish a sentence or not have a point to what they were saying, Yes, And did it drive you crazy, Yes, Well that is a wonderful way to hijack someones mind to plant hypnotic suggestions in them, You can walk up to someone and say something like I have been meaning to talk to you about something and then just drop the subject.

And start talking about some insignificant something and you will be able to see it in there eyes that they are no longer listening to you there mind is concentrating on what you did not say, while you are babbling on drop in a few hypnotic suggestions, They will go straight to the subconscious mind while they are in this daze, This is just another form of conversational hypnosis and it works like a charm, Every time.

There are thousands of ways to do this and I can not possibly go through all of them so you must use your imagination and just start doing, Another quick one is, Tell a joke that has no punch line and then laugh at it, There mind will immediate begin the process of reviewing the joke trying to figure out if they missed something, Now is the time place your suggestions NOW, Works every time.

Quick inductions such as the handshake induction work on a shock method, If you reach out to give someone a hand shake, They are expecting a regular everyday hand shake, If you do something that does not register with them as normal it throws there mind into a what tha bull, kinda swirl and you simply say sleep, And they sleep, No you just cannot go out and start doing this it takes practice to get the timing right but it almost always works, This goes back to what I was telling you about bypassing the conscious mind.

Anytime you busy the conscious mind it leaves the subconscious open to you, And all you have to do is think up diabolical ways to use this split second of time you have bought yourself and continue into there subconscious, Remember when I told you the subconscious (Just Does) it does not have the ability to reason why it just simple does, Once yo are speaking directly to the subconscious you can tell it to do things and it will just do them, Such as sleep.

They are not really asleep like you think of sleep they are in a state of awe or in a state of shock for lack of a better way to put it, It amazes me that you could put everything that I have every learned in my life into a thimble but when it comes to explaining how I got to know it or why the things I know work, All of a sudden I can fill up a book it is ridicules.

There is a lot of trickery going on in hypnosis and more so when you leave off the long inductions, Because hypnosis can happen so fast, When I first tried a quick induction and it was the handshake, I was so shocked myself that the person just fell over onto my shoulder awaiting instruction that I had none, I had not trusted it to work so I had not thought past that part of the whole deal and I had to go right into a wake up speech to make sure that they had not effects left over from being tranced, It was very embarrassing and I don't want it to happen to you and you for sure don't want it to happen to you, So the reason I am telling you this is why practice practice practice before you go out and do something and be left looking like an idiot, All inductions you see on the Internet or in books or where ever else you may get your information work, At some time or another. they worked for somebody and thats not hard to believe because hypnosis.

Hypnosis is not (Fragile) things you do not think will work, Will work and leave you standing there looking like a fool if you are not ready for it.

Do not fall into the trap of expecting something not to work be ready for it to work, Expect it to work, Be prepared to catch a person if they begin to fall and some will, Be ready for anything, Be ready for an adverse reaction to be tranced, That no one on Gods wonderful earth has ever seen before be ready for anything because, Anything is exactly is what may happen, I am not saying be afraid to trance someone but take on the responsibility of being ready for when they are, Do not let someone who trust you be hurt because you are not ready for what may happen.

When you use a quick trance if the person is standing have your hand on them so that you can pull them into you if necessary to keep them from falling, If they are sitting keep a hand on them for balance and guide them into a SAFE stable place, Do not allow them to move into any position that might hurt them, I have had a broken back unnatural positions can lead to me having to go through month's of rehab and a whole; e lot of pain and grief.

If you are the unlucky person that causes this to happen to me I am going to sue you, And there are many people out there with worse attitudes that I have, But know if you hurt me it is going to cost you money, And the world is full of people like me attitude wise and health wise also so you must be careful with everything you do, And having malpractice insurance is important to if you plan to do this for a living, Thing is just do not hurt anyone all it takes is a little thought to be ready for just about anything so make sure you do this.

I am going to put the hypnotist ethics in the back of the book and I think it would be a good time to skip ahead and read them, By teaching people how to do something I do not want to unleash a bunch of untrained bumpkins loses on society, Hypnosis van be a safe thing just as driving a car but there is always the exception to every rule when something seemingly safe is taken into the wrong hands, Of people who do not care about anyone but there self, I suggest after you finish this book you get some instruction Somewhere

It just so happens that I have classes that teach hypnosis and get you certified but if not me then someone this book is not in anyway get you ready for all the tings you may run into out there doing this for a living so get more instruction somewhere, I am not a very good writer I know that, I am like everyone else I have something to say that may or may not help someone with there future, But I know I am not a good written and I am not a very patient instructor either but the fact that I am a perfectionist gives me an edge when teaching people to do something because I will not settle for second best.

If you get instruction from me in a class room you be good and you will be careful and considerate of others or you will be gone that is up to you, Alright I am going to get off this kick now and tell you more ways to trick the conscious and leave the subconscious wide open for whatever, When a person reaches out to shake your hand put your other hand on there wrist and pull there hand to there face and tell them to look closely at it and say sleep and pull there head towards your shoulder and deepen right away, This works almost completely by catching them off guard, Speed is the major thing, Don t rattle so fast they freak out, But quickly and firmly speck in a slow but steady line of works the moment you stop talking is the moment you will lose them remember shock is your friend when using technique's like this.

I will post complete speed inductions toward the end of the book the problem is that almost everyone uses the same ones and that leads others to believe you are coping there work and I don't like to feel like I copy anyone I am perfectly able to come up with new ones on my own but will they work for you, I do not know that is why I like posting tried and tested methods, But everyone has a different personality, What I mean is I come off as a very intimidating person so I in turn have to be careful how I do these things, Or I will get the wrong reaction where as a less threating person might do great with a lot of touching, But fact is If I start touching people I have just met all over there body I will wind up in jail. Hypnotizing inmates not to have sex with me.

So everything about your personality comes into play when you are dealing with perfect strangers, But so what all you want to do is get into there head anyway you do not have to look a certain way to do that you just have to be smart, So lets figure out how to get into every person we meets head for exercise, Really think about it when you meet new people, I do.

There is the eye contact induction it is hard to do and sometimes the person takes this for a treat so I do not recommend it but if you want to use it it will be in the end of the book, Fact is they are all the same once you know how they work inductions are for people who really have no imagination because once you practice these things for a bit you will realize that it does not have to be a particular way you do something every time it is the end results and you can ghetto those a thousand different ways, So what I would like you to do is to look at everything you see, And then ask yourself why and how it works.

This is important because you do not have to do things like every body else does, Yes it is good when you are just starting out but it you give everything you do some thought once you realize how it is done you have found your freedom to be unique.

There can make as much money as you want to make selling hypnosis videos on the Internet, Thats is what it is about for most people and I do respect the fact that we all need money, I like to help people that is what it is about for me, If you help someone in distress for free and make your money on the Internet then hey I respect you, And I would think that you are an asset to the world, At this point I am just rambling I have told you every thing you need to know about this hypnosis thing, It is up to you to make it work, Just remember you do not have to do it just exactly like everyone else does it you have a mind and I am sure you can take what I have already told you and make this stuff work, Without being there to hands on teach you there is not much else I can do except post the inductions in this book and put my twist on them so here we go.

5 CHAPTER

INDUCTIONS JUST LIKE EVERYONE ELSE'S

Lets practice Inductions for a bit, Remember it is the simple things that will work best for you be relaxed and confident, When you are starting a induction adjust your breathing to be as close as you can to your clients this helps relax them and it is all about relaxation, I told you they do not really go to sleep just a deep state of relaxation, So everything you do to make them more comfortable the better.

After each induction I am going to mention ways that work better for me, Is that OK, Well of course it is it is my book right, I am going to start with some Dave Elman inductions some say he is the fastest hypnotist in the whole wide world I do not know about that but he is a very good hypnotist.

We can all be very fast hypnotist, If the people we are working with have been conditioned before hand, So to me this should not count, After I have hypnotized someone I always leave a suggestion in there mind to go quickly back into trance for the sound of my voice and for me period really, Which means I can actually run unto these people years later and say the right words and have them back into trance in about 3 seconds.

Why you are going to ask, Well it goes back to the fact that I told you the subconscious takes a kind of picture of everything that happens to you in your life and files it away, RIGHT, Now what does that mean it means that even if he or she has completely forgotten me, When I say the trigger word that there subconscious mind rolls threw all the files up there in there head and goes right back to the moment, Them there mind reacts the way I told it to when I called on it again.

So there, When working with a pre conditioned person it is nothing to get right back into trance, So anyone that has ever been hypnotized before even by someone else is more subject to fall right back into a trance again, This is also the theory of how spies are supposed to be somewhere just waiting to be awoken by the right word from anyone, Sleepers are very well possible, But what saves us in that situation is that they cannot be made to do anything that they are morally against.

Because why I told you this also, Your conscious mind will stop them from doing it, Why because it goes against what they believe in, Now can there be sleepers of this sort, Yes it is possible but I will say this, They would have to be terrible people anyway and have no morals or they would have had to have been convinced that what they were doing was a good thing, And yes I do believe that there are skilled people out there that are tested enough to go through all this trouble to do this to someone. Absolutely.

Now back to the induction, until I have another thought or wish to make a statement, OK thats enough for a minute the induction I am looking at is a count down induction which is similar to a stairway induction and I in no way have the patients for these, I do not like them for myself but I will post it because it is very effective and they work great, As a matter of fact it is a great induction for a beginner because they very often work, My problem is that I fall into a real deep sleep myself trying to deliver one, But I am about to post it for all of you.

Here we go Induction Below:

Before you begin going into your hypnotic trance now just make yourself comfortable.

Just settle yourself down and you can relax now. All you have to do is to focus on becoming comfortable.

Take a moment now and wiggle about until you are in the right position for what comes Next

(Let Them Take A few Moments To Get Comfortable)

Look around your body and notice if there is any tightness, or any discomfort, and maybe just shrug everything until you are happily settled down and ready. If anything is making you uncomfortable then fix it.

Fixing things stops them bothering you doesn't it?

Now, in a moment I am going to count down from ten to one, and when I get to one you will have relaxed into a deep satisfying trance. But before that you can move every part of your body as you become loose and floppy and relaxed.

Now take a deep breath and relax it. Just let it all flow out... ahhhhh. That's right.

Now tense up your whole body, and then let go again... really relax... and feel

how good that is...

TEN... focus your attention on your feet ... think about your feet... think about

letting your feet and toes and ankles relax and get loose.

NINE... Now relax all the muscles in your legs... in you calves, your knees your thighs... very relaxed... feel those legs getting heavy and heavier...

EIGHT... now feel that relaxation spreading into your body... your chest....

SEVEN... and now feel that relaxation in your shoulders... spreading all the way

down your arms... down to you hands... your fingers... and those arms feel so

heavy... so relaxed... it is as if they belong to someone else...

SIX... and now allow your neck to relax... and become aware of your face

relaxing... your cheeks... your jaw... your lips ...

FIVE... let your eyes relax... your eyebrows...your forehead...

FOUR... and everything feels loose and heavy... as if you arms and legs were

made of stone... totally relaxed... you can feel the weight pressing down... and

you just can't move those arms and legs now... and you can enjoy this feeling of

total relaxation... letting go... and the more you relax the more you can relax...

THREE... and as your mind drifts off you feel a wave of relaxation traveling down

your body ... down and down... from the top of your head... relaxing your face...

relaxing your neck... your shoulders your body... spreading... down and down...

gently and easily... feel your body sinking down... safe and warm and secure...

TWO... and each soft gentle breath out... is relaxing you more... and that relaxing

means you can relax deeper and deeper now... letting go... drifting away...

nothing matters... enjoying that that lovely feeling...

ONE... and totally relaxed now... totally at ease... and your mind can drift away to

a place... far, far away.... a place where you feel relaxed... where you feel

comfortable... always... and think of what the place is like... what other places

there might be that you make you feel comfortable... maybe a beach at twilight...

or a favorite chair... or snuggled warm in bed on a stormy night... or maybe

floating in warm water... allow your mind to drift over these things and other

things... whatever feels right for you... as you drift ever deeper... enjoying the

feeling ... nothing matters... nothing is important... just being in the moment...

let your mind empty...

Ok This is me again .... Now you must do a few deepeners here and there because

this alone is not enough to get them in a trance and keep them there.

That induction you just read comes in many forms but they all do the same thing, I seldom ever even try to do an induction just as it is written you will find as you get more experience, That trying to follow something that someone else wrote can make you nervous and that is not good again Hypnosis is not a fragile thing, You do not have to try and go word for word with something someone else wrote, Also you will find is that when you are trying to do something someone else wrote it kind of hard to do, Which makes you stress a bit and the stress will show in your voice and that is worse than making a mistake on the induction.

The best was to do this is make sure you look at these inductions as a suggestion, They are not wrote in stone and it will not hurt anything if you mess one up, With a tiny bit of quick thinking you can recover from a mistake, Or even better you can just pretend it never even happened and go on with what you were doing.

You will do more damage than good trying to fix a mistake so just move on with your induction, All jokes a side this is a great induction for beginners, It is easy to do, And it works about every time, Sometimes things do not work for different reasons, Some people just have it in there head that they cannot be hypnotized,

If they just think that you can hypnotize them anyway but when you are just starting out it is not worth your time and also dealing with people with this kind of

attitude can hurt your EGO and you do not need that when you are beginning, Try and stay with people who are eager to be hypnotized at first then you can move on to the people that have issues, The above was a good induction you can practice this and kind of make it your own them when you try to use it you will be comfortable with it.

I am going to move right now to another induction. Also for general information no one owns the patent on these inductions, Many of them were wrote by people long ago that are no longer with us, One of the greatest hypnotist of all times wrote many scripts and he gave many of the technique's that people today use and his name was Milton Erickson his family owns a lot of his works and his theories and such as that, But most all the rest do not belong to anyone, They are an idea of how to do something and they can be changed and adjusted to work best for the person using them, In other words they are no more than a suggestion or a method and in time if you stay with this kind of work you will develop your own methods that work for you, Just as I have.

We are going to look at the staircase induction now, And I wonder if you can imagine a big old house somewhere?.....

.... with a fence... and a big garden... and maybe there are trees....

... it's the sort of house that families grew up in... generations of people.... living and laughing.....

....There's been weddings and parties... Christmas trees and Easter Eggs... and birthday candles and happy times....

...inside that house... there's a staircase....

....And you can find yourself at the top of that staircase....

...and I don't know if that staircase is wood or marble... or carpet.... doesn't matter.....

...and there can be a handrail....

...and you can imagine yourself beginning to go down those steps.... safe and secure... comfortable.... because at the bottom there is a door....

... and behind that door is a wonderful thing, for you.

... and you can begin to go down those steps now ... and with every step you get more relaxed.... and deeper into trance and so

TEN going down.... deeper relaxed... and NINE deeper still.....

... and EIGHT.... deeper relaxed...

...and SEVEN... down and down...

.... and SIX...

And feel yourself sinking into that chair... wonderfully supported as if you are lying on a fleecy cloud ... just allowing yourself to drift.....

...and FIVE.... deeper and deeper.....

...and FOUR .... down and down....

... and THREE....

....and TWO....

...and there is one step left....

... and when you go down from that last step.... there is just zero....and you can

imagine drifting through the center of that zero.... through a black void of

nothingness... a wonderful soft velvety warm comfortable darkness.... you are

relaxed and at ease... your mind is completely relaxed....

...and the only thing of importance is the sound of my voice... everything else can

fade away...

Next Induction and then a comment:

ESCALATOR hypnosis INDUCTION

And it's odd for me to think of you sitting there now.... just breathing gently...

wondering about... how easily.... how quickly.... you can go into that lovely

relaxed state...

and while wondering... maybe you can imagine someone just like you... some other person wanting to go into that relaxed dreamy state.... and how you could help that person into that state of comfort... of quiet relaxation.... and you might imagine saying to that person... become aware of your breathing... of how your breath moves gently in and out... and tell them... how on every breath out ... you can relax a little more ... and just rest for a few moments.... and allow time to relax... deeply... completely... and notice how that relaxation progresses... smoothly...

... and then get them to imagine a quiet, peaceful spot... maybe on a warm

afternoon.... to imagine lying comfortably... somewhere nice.... mind drifting

away... imagine arms and legs.... eyelids... are beginning to feel tired and

heavy... as heavy as lead.... to relax ... totally... to just let things go... and drift

away....

...and now imagine being at the top of an escalator... a moving staircase....

looking down.... and allow them to be carried down that escalator... safely and

securely.... carried gently down and down... more deeply relaxed... as that

escalator goes down.. carried deeper and deeper... the body relaxes more.... and

your mind relaxes more.... going deeper and deeper with every comfortable

breath... and by and by you are drifting off into an endless velvety welcoming

dreamland...

Alright as I said before before we started this they are all pretty much alike, This

is just another example of the same induction I will post another and I feel that

should be sufficient for you to start writing your own. Them we will move to

deepens and other things.

Emotional Release Induction

Good... that's good.... and now take a deep breath.... ahhhh... and another deep

breath... and one more deep breath... and just allow the whole of your body to

relax... that's good

Now that you are relaxing.... you can allow your mind to change things for you...

you can use the inner power that is in all of us...

and I want you to imagine that inner power.... and just for a moment allow your

eyes to close .. that's right....

and as you lie there... relaxing... I wonder if you can imagine some dark dim

place somewhere... some place safe and warm and comfortable...

and imagine there is a speck of light... and imagine that speck of light moving...

and imagine that speck of light guiding you safely down... and down... and as

that speck of light moves you feel yourself drawn down and

down....

and thinking about that speck of light... you can feel your body slowing down...

your eyes getting heavy.... and the weight of your arms and legs... feel your arms

and legs getting tired and heavy... imagine the whole of your body getting heavy

and tired... and relaxing... deeper and deeper now....

imagine going deeper into that dark place... as that speck leads you on... gliding

further down... imagine your body sinking... drifting... deeper and deeper...

and feel yourself relaxing... easing... sinking... like going down into the deep dark

blue waters of the ocean...

feel yourself slowly, gently... following that speck... deeper and deeper... more

and more relaxed... and imagine that speck of light is leading you through a long

dim corridor... and as you go down that corridor...

every sound you hear makes you even more relaxed... allows you to drift even

deeper.... and all around you... things are becoming quiet and peaceful... and

every sound becomes soothing and gentle and every sound is leading you down

and down as you relax those sounds right out of your mind... everything is disappearing....

and just thinking about that speck of light... imagine it now spreading soft gentle

light everywhere... feel yourself wrapped in that light... cocooned... held gently

safely... drifting away... supported by that light...

soft and indistinct... like a quiet glow.... as it softly spreads out further and

further... you feel yourself somehow spreading... easing.... letting go.... feel

yourself going deeper and with each passing moment....

the feeling comes over you that nothing really matters now... as you relax more

and more deeply... you feel that you don't really care any more... just letting

everything go...

and just feel yourself relaxing completely... letting go... deeper and deeper...

that's right....

Alright I have a ton of ground to cover so we are moving on to the next chapter

which will cover many different thing, We shall see where it takes us.

6 CHAPTER

COMBINATION OF MEDITATION & HYPNOSIS

OK That was that and I have had about all I want of induction, Now I want to give you the confidence and the knowledge just to write your own or even better to not need one, You do not need an induction once you understand what they do and how they do it, First what do all of these induction have in common, Other than they are all designed to relax a person, They are all repetitious but thats still not the important thing, If you look close at them you will see that deep breathing is very important, Why, Because the oxygen relaxes you.

Another thing is the tone of the hypnotist voice it must be a sort of a lullaby to the clients it must be soft and pleasing to bring on relaxation. You could say just about anything and if you said it right it would be very relaxing, Another thing is trust your clients must trust you, Beyond trusting you enough to be in a closed room with you they must trust you with there secrets and they must trust you to help them.

It is like when you go to the doctor you know what ever he does may just be painful but after he is done you will begin to get relief, These are all major things to consider when learning to hypnotize,Anytime you feel you are losing your client have them take another deep long breath, It calms them down right away, Then go back to your induction, Another important thing is to never stop telling them how good they are doing, For instance I have to go through some very very agonizing shots for my back but the doctor is always telling me I am doing good, He is reassuring me that everything is fine.

You get the same thing from the dentist what is he always telling you, He is always telling you that you are doing good, That is a form of hypnosis all in itself,

You are doing good, Simple but very effective, And I know when they stick me in the back with a 4 inch needle I cannot hear it enough and that is the truth.

I really wish I could talk to the people as they read this book because I keep wanting to say things like well what did you get out of that and why do you think that happened or why did that work, Well I am looking for scripts that I can take apart to see what makes them work but I am not liking what I am finding, I guess we will play with deepeners for awhile, Well maybe one more script, No lets talk awhile about what hypnosis and meditation have in common, That is worth writing about, Can you guys believe you actually payed for me to ramble on like this.

Amazing and thank God for America and his grace, Alright lets move on, Let me jump clean off the bridge here and say before we get started that nothing is an accident, I have been seriously hurt a few times way to many really I was in 12 motorcycle accidents in one year so I know what I am talking about, God built us with a certain fail safe built right into us and it is called shock for one thing.

When you are in serious pain, And yes I mean the kind you get when you wreck a motorcycle, There is something in your mind that makes you numb, Not forever I can attest to that but right then when it first happens you get numb, No pain, And we can do this with hypnosis also, I look at things such as the universe and I realize how wonderful God is and how wonderful his creations are, If you think about it the earth is replenishing itself all the time.

Everything about it is just wonderful, Yes there is a point to this,

Man is constantly looking for how things work it is in our nature to do so, And we are learning at warp speed, Hypnosis and the mind are no different man is trying his best to find out everything about how it works, And hypnosis is one of those things that really still needs a lot of research because we do not really know everything we could know about how it works.

But we take what we do know about it and we utilize it to our advantage, Such as controlling chronic pain with hypnosis.

I suffer every day from chronic pain and it is no picnic, But it has brought me to look in places I would have never looked without the pain, Such as hypnosis, I got interested in hypnosis as a way to control my own pain and I have had wonderful results from it, But I still search for that spot like I said before, Like just after an accident when there is no pain, I am looking for that for myself, I have found it for others but I so far have not been able to find it for myself, I will keep looking but the pain has driving me to get a degree in physiology that I don't really even use.

Well I do but I have no desire to be a physiologist, But this is why I feel meditation is so important to us, Meditation is different from hypnosis, And we can use it to conquer just about anything that comes our way.

So I would like all of you to do as much research as you can into meditation also, I feel that you are all outstanding smart people after all you were all smart enough to buy this book.

And I feel you all have so much to offer yourselves and the world I want to urge you to learn all you can about meditation and use it daily with your hypnosis because you can do just about anything with it, I see so many people out there that have so many different kinds of problems that I know can be fixed with meditation, The first thing is confidence, Everyone should have all the confidence they can without becoming cocky, It will drive you in your life to knew places.

Never let anyone tell you that you are not smart enough to do anything because you are smart enough to do anything you put your mind to, And there we are again put your mind too, Well hypnosis and meditation can help you put your mind into the things you want out of life and everyone deserves to be happy, The first thing however that you must do before anything will start happening in your life is to make peace with what you already have.

Before you can begin to attracting new things into your life you must find comfort in the things you already have, Once you are happy and thankful with what you have will you open yourself up to attracting more, And yes they do just come to like magic, You can look at what is going on in your life and say well this would happen if I did this and I did that.

Well you are wrong you do not have to do much of anything at all, And no I do not mean just stop everything and wait for good things to happen you must continue to strive for the things you want out

of life, But until you find happiness with the things you have anything more would

just be wasted on you and that my friends is a fact, Get into the mindset that you thank God everyday for things like breathing and heart beats and the fact that you slept indoors last night, If you have a car be thankful for the car you have, Yes even if it is a 1972 Pinto, and if you have insurance on it be thankful for that, and if it has gas in it be thankful for that, Be grateful if you have someone in the world that loves you and I am not just talking about hot girls.

Be thankful for every moment you are able to spend with your family, Be thankful that you are loved by the people that you are loved by and be thankful for the love that God has for you and when you can do these things, A wealth of things will just start coming your way, Doors will start opening for you that you never thought was possible ever in your life.

We bring about the things that happen to use in life by our mindset and our actions towards others and meditation can help you with all of these things, It has been said that life is an illusion brought about by you and this is true in many ways, Life can be very fulfilling to you in so many more ways than it is right now but you must be worthy of its good graces, The most important thing is how you treat others, The good news is yes you can manipulate your life it is not only possible it is pretty easy,

You begin with your actions and continue from there, Yes I know there are a whole bunch of you sitting there right this very moment going well I never done nothing to nobody in my whole life, Maybe thats the problem, Maybe it is time you done something to somebody and something for somebody too while you are at it.

There are many ways out there that work that are based on power of the mind, I am not going to mention them by name because I am tired of being sued and you never know what some will do, But meditation is what they are all based on meditation, The proper mindset is necessary to bring more into your life.

Visualizing the things you want out of life is a great way to begin attracting better stuff into you life, There are many programs out there that will without a doubt help you, I am going to begin a program of my own soon so if by some strange reason you like my wacky ways look for me, Life has been very very good to me and I want to help others as much as I can find there dreams, Creative visualizing is a wonderful way to do this, Also you must change your mindset to where you expect great things to come your way every second of everyday and they will.

I would like for everyone reading this book to stop reading right this minute and get on the Internet and find a good free meditation program and you will find that I am right about everything I am saying.

The first thing you need to do is meditate on how grateful you are for the things you already have in your life, Once you are grateful for what you have you will be blessed with tons of wonderful things to be grateful about, Be thankful for everything be thankful for every heart beat, For every breath you take, For every bite of food you chew and swallow, Find things to be grateful about, And you will see once you get into this mindset things will just start flowing into your life, But the first thing you must do is make your life fit for new things and you do this by being happy with the things you have, If you give a child a gift and he throws on the floor and wants another one do you want to give him another one.

Of course you don't.

Once you get happy with the things you have better things will be coming soon, Look for them expect them, But never ever think you deserve them, That is a mistake to ever think you deserve better, You don't, Everything in life happens for a reason and if you think long enough and hard enough you will understand what put you where you are in life, Circumstances are created by actions, Your actions, And if you want to get better results from life you must change the things that got you where you are in life right now.

The good news is that you can change everything that needs changing about your life, Just take one small step at a

time, Don't try to change everything in one day just change one small thing at a time and you will be shocked at the things that start going your way.

Effort in the right direction will bring on a supernatural advancements from places you never thought possible all of a sudden people you never thought were interested will all of a sudden get interested in what you are doing, When you think you are not capable of changing anything that matters in the world you have over looked something and that something is you, When you start to change yourself everything that has anything at all to do with you will begin to change also and it can make a movement that can change the world, And at the very least it can and will change your world and that is a fact, So start to meditate tonight and don't worry so much about how you can change the world.

Just adapt to the world and watch it begin to bless you with things you never even knew you needed. When I said earlier about you being able to help others by using Nlp you can, What I said earlier about you can make great someones life with hypnosis you can, You can bring about miracle's in a persons life just by changing there mindset about life as a hole, You should not meddle in another persons life but from now on when you look at a person don't try and figure what they are doing wrong look at them and think what can I do to help them do better, I am teaching you how to change a persons mind lets take that a little farther if you care enough you can change there whole life, And maybe just everyone in there life.

Lets think about the ripple effect, I don't know if there is really anything to what the person wrote that brought that up but let us just take that name the ripple effect and think about it, And lets think about it from a point we can all relate to, Our children, Is that not a ripple from our being alive, Well yes it is. We must think about everything from the stand point of how it effects others, When I started to grow up a little in my thinking it was after hurricane Katrina.

When I saw the bodies that had to have someones family just floating along in the water from the floods, I thought it was the worst things that I had ever seen and it in fact was, And then they jumped over to the police marching across the bridge threating to kill people if they did not move back and I thought to myself how could they be so cruel, And after giving it an enormous amount of thought I came to realize that they had done what they had to do for the greater good.

Even if they had have had to kill one or two people to feed the many that is what they had to do, The greater good, Well without thinking of others how can you expect to be granted more in this world, The world is not all about you it is about every living soul in it, Before we can expect more out of life we have to learn about the things we already have in life because if we do not appreciate those what good would it do for us to have more from a karmic stand point.

Back to the ripple affect for a minute, Everything we have ever done in our life has impacted many people, Weather we will believe it or not, The way we treat others and our children even more so has a great impact on the whole world not just myself and my kids, The kids that they have and the kids after that, If you are flawed in the things you do, The there are consequence's to it, I began this book about hypnosis and the mind because that is what I know the most about.

But thats not all that is important it is everything about life that will make a difference in your life and the lives of others and with meditation you can make a huge change in everyones life and yes I believe even people you do not know.

Self hypnosis can also make a huge and wonderful change in your life, It works and brings about the same results as meditation but in some cases works much faster, To get you back into the trade I am going to give you a whole lot of information on self hypnosis and meditation and then I am going to give you some deepeners for when you hypnotize others and then this book is done.

I have been merely giving you some things in my opinion are worthwhile for you to do exercises in, And I really have a hard time sticking to one subject but every word I have written in this has been very good information although I may never sell another book after this I have had fun, Also at the end of the book you will begiven contact information to get in touch with me to discuss any of the many things we have gone over in here.

Norman Bowman C.Ht

7 CHAPTER
SELF HYPNOSIS IS GOOD TOO

Right at this very second I am going to go out on a limb and put a bunch of information about self hypnosis and meditation in here for your learning pleasure.

Meditation has many characteristics similar to hypnosis. They both are attempts to reach the many qualities of the subconscious mind, Weather or not you ever get anything more from self hypnosis or meditation you will find that it relaxes you and renews you in ways not much else can do, So your attempts at self hypnosis or meditation will not be UN fruitful you will find that they better your life even when your attempts do not get you all the way where you want to be, I strongly suggest weather you make it or not on your first attempts you do not give up because the relaxation benefits are spectacular so do not give up.

There are mp3's out there you can get to guide you and help you on your way I have used those and they are good if you get them from a good source I have not as yet tried to make any tapes or dvd's not that I won't sooner or later I just have not wanted to buy the software needed and there is also the thing about me having a very strong southern drawl, I find it attractive coming from a woman I find it offensive and degrading coming from myself.

There is also that thing about everyone thinking that anyone with a southern accent is stupid too, The self hypnosis script below I take no credit for I got it from the Internet and it said and I quot use at will I however did see a name in the credits and I am placing it here, I would like to also add that I think it is very good work and if you are looking for more you should without a doubt Google this man's name and see if you can get more of this wonderful quality. The name I found associated with this work is : The "blue sky" part is based on a meditation in David Fontana's

book The Meditator's Handbook :

When you listen to this recording, please make sure that you're somewhere where it's safe to ignore the environment for a while and completely relax.

You can listen to it sitting or lying down. A good time is just before you fall asleep at night; if you find you fall asleep before the recording finishes, try sitting up instead of lying down.

Get into a comfortable position, arms and legs uncrossed. We're going to start by taking three deep breaths, and as you take each deep breath in, you'll be taking in relaxation, and as you let it slowly out, you'll be letting out any tension. OK,

First deep breath in… hold it for a moment… and out, and let go, relax. Second deep breath in… hold it… let go, relax. Third deep breath… hold it… let go, relax.

If you haven't already done so, you can let your eyelids gently drift closed.

Now imagine that you're lying somewhere that you really like, lying on your back where you can see the sky, or sitting if you prefer. It might be a meadow full of wildflowers, or a beach, or a raft on a calm lake, or a clearing among the trees, or a garden or park. Somewhere that you're comfortable and relaxed. You're breathing easily, looking up into a beautiful deep blue sky, a cloudless blue sky.

You can't see the sun from this angle but the sun is shining and there's a pleasant breeze, so you're very comfortable and relaxed. And as you lie there looking up into the depths of the blue sky, that very calm, blue, open sky, relaxing more and more, you feel lighter and lighter, and in a very safe and pleasant way you begin to feel as if you're drifting, as if gravity is loosening its hold on you and you're beginning to float upwards like a balloon, floating gently into the blue sky.

You're very calm and peaceful, it's a pleasant, safe sensation, a sensation of freedom as you float and drift gently upwards into the deep blue sky.

Soon all you can see is the blueness surrounding you, and a calm sensation fills

you as you continue to breathe slowly and deeply, relaxing more and more as

you're gradually absorbed, gently absorbed into the blueness and the

peacefulness. It fills you and you fill it, becoming one with the blue sky, peaceful,

calm and relaxed.

And in the way that things happen in dreams, there's a gentle shift from looking

into the blue sky to looking into a calm, peaceful, beautiful deep blue sea. And

you can breathe quite easily and naturally, because dream logic applies. Far below

through the clear, calm blue water you can see the soft, sandy bottom of the sea,

and that represents the deepest level of relaxation that you can imagine.

And as I count slowly from 1 to 10, you can just allow yourself to naturally drift

down, gently and calmly, quietly and safely, to that very deep level of relaxation.

One, drifting and floating. Two, calmly and quietly. Three, safely held by the

water. Four, just drifting. Five, gently and naturally. Six, easily and pleasantly.

Seven, deeper and deeper. Eight, so peaceful, so relaxed. Nine, approaching that

deep level. And ten, just gently, calmly, coming to rest at that very deep level of

relaxation. And you may find as you continue to allow your body and mind to be

very relaxed, that you will drift even deeper as the words wash over you and as

you experience a very deep and pleasant relaxed calm state.

And in that peaceful, calm, relaxed state, the part of your mind which looks after

your habitual thoughts, feelings and behaviors becomes much more accessible

and able to be communicated with, so you can tell it about any changes that you

want to make that will be for your benefit as a whole person. And the creativity of

that subconscious mind is well able to find solutions to meet all your needs as a

whole person, without needing thoughts or feelings or behaviors that may have

been distressing you or causing you problems. So just drift now for a few

minutes, as long as you need but you only need a few minutes, to let your subconscious find those solutions. You don't have to consciously know what they are; you'll just find your life changing for the better. And when you've had long enough, just return to your usual alert state, feeling calm, peaceful and relaxed.

I felt as if this was a wonderful piece of work and I also used it so I suppose that is the highest compliment that I can give it, I used it, Next up a meditation or so and then onward.

There is a difference between hypnosis and meditation but it is not a lot.

Meditation and hypnosis are similar both will bring forth a deep state of relaxation but there are differences in the fact that when you use self hypnosis if you go about it that way you end up dealing with the subconscious mind, They have somewhat different purposes also and it is my feelings that you need both and you should use both on a daily basis to balance your life out, Also there are many different forms of meditation such as mantra where they use chanting.

All I am going to say on this is you need to look at yourself I certainly do not think there is anything wrong with this form of meditation it is just not for me, Also the chanting interferes with the total relaxation that I get from meditating.

Some people stare at different objects to bring on there relaxation again not for me, I want my eyes closed when I am meditating on a subject or thinking about life in general, But a lot of these methods I have never used so I will not condemn something especially if I have not done it also it may be that it is right up your ally so I say give it a try if you want to.

Fact is they are so much alike that if you sat two people side by side, one in hypnosis and one in meditation, it would be hard to say which person was in hypnosis and which one was meditating, As far as I can tell meditation is just another means of entering the hypnotic state. I am a born again Christian and I find that meditation is alright as a matter of the bible says in it many times to meditate, The act of meditation is often linked with a certain set spiritual beliefs.

While this differs greatly from hypnosis, they both invoke altered states through concentration and are actually quite similar. Hypnosis and meditation can each be used to eliminate physical discomfort, However, The belief in the spiritual aspect of meditation and the deepening of that connection is a benefit that lies solely in the realm of meditation. I wouldn't suggest hypnosis as a great way of strengthening your spirituality or embarking on a spiritual journey, Meditation might not be the best way to resolve emotional conflicts or stop unwanted behaviors. So while there is certainly some common ground, the purpose and personal use of each can be quite unique.

So I am going to strongly suggest meditation for a centered life and as a way to refresh yourself, Once you get good at meditation you will be able to use it in a very short period of time to catch some quick or badly needed rest and when you are done you will be refreshed, The tings I am telling you about in this book are not just something I decided to write about to make a few bucks because lord knows I am not that good at writing. But Praise God My Books Keep Selling

But most of the things I am going over in this book are important to live a good life, I am 56 years old and if I had have been in touch with things like this when I was younger I can tell you honestly that I would have had a much better life, And also that since I have found these things that my life has greatly improved and I want that for others, I really do care.

Weather or not this book is successful I will be writing more and maybe just maybe my writing skills will improve but weather or not I get to be a better writer I feel as if it helps even one person live a better life it is worth it to me, Another thing is I am going back and tell you more about creative visualization because it is very important to you no matter what you do for a living, or what situation you are in now because your situation can always get better and the fact that is that everyone should be happy that is a God given right.

This is a another meditation practice that should help you get started .With both meditation or hypnosis, You can use your talent to set this one up.

CHAPTER 9
DEEP ENER'S

Follow the basic physical and mental relaxation technique from here.

When you have done this then do the following:

Say " I will countdown from 10 down to 1 and with each descending number I will

relax more and more". Then say " 10, I am relaxing more and more, 9, I am

relaxing more and more…" and so on all the way down to one. This serves as a

mental anchor (link) associating a 10-1 count down with deep relaxation. You

could also imagine standing at a staircase of 10 steps and each step down makes

you more and more relaxed (in this method imagine taking each step down after

you say the number). You could also imagine that you are writing each number

on a blackboard and erasing it for the next one. Whatever works best for you.

When you have done your 10-1 countdown after your basic relaxation practice you are in a very relaxed state of mind and body. At this point

you could set your anchor using three fingers of either hand (by pressing

them together, lightly).

You could also do one of the visualization techniques to create an even better

inner state and anchor that state. You can set the anchor as many times as you

like i.e. after each technique you do. This will make your anchor very strong.

Later when you need to access calm, confident and happy states of mind all you

will have to do is press your three fingers together (triggering your anchor), take

a deep breath and imagine your chosen peaceful scene. That's it. Instant stress

relief.

When you are done relaxing, anchoring, affirmations and

visualizations and are ready to end your meditation/self-hypnosis

practice do a 1-5 'count up'. This counting also serves as an anchor for

you as you get used to becoming fully alert and aware at the end of it:

Start by saying, "I am going to count from 1 to 5 and with each ascending

number I will become more alert and aware ready and able to have a wonderful day/evening. then start by saying "1 more alert and aware, 2 feeling refreshed

and re energized, 3, ….5, alert and feeling wonderfully refreshed". Open your eyes

when you say 5 then say the last affirmation are you're done.

One more of these and moving on, You should be able to use these for templates and make your own after this, If not there is a wealth of thesefree on the Internet.

When trying to learn to meditate, you will find that your mind will wanders and thoughts will ''pop in'' to your head. Those thoughts will try to distract you. Your mind ''chattering'' with thoughts is a common occurrence when learning mediation. At first, your mind is like an undisciplined child and the ''monkey mind''(as we sometimes call it) will hamper your training IF you let it bother you. So what can you do about it?

Don't get frustrated! That is vital. As soon as you notice a lapse in attention or concentration, simply re-focus. Immediately redirect your mind back, and continue or begin again. Be patient with your self rather than falling into the trap of blaming or getting angry with yourself, or getting frustrated - which can lead to giving up.

Maybe of interest to you.

Mirroring someone movements can get them into a trance, I have never tried this one, But mirroring to a certain extent can bring them to feel comfortable with you and it is used as a way to hypnotize someone, But it will help a reason warm up to you, And it helps to make a person feel safe around you, The reason this works is it makes a person feel a bond with you, And it also makes they feel not alone, And safe with you, It is a physiological effect of being like another.

Not feeling alone, Feeling a kinship with another party, Yes all just because you mimic there movements a little. You can use this method with the leader of a group to make them feel as if you belong with them, And it also makes them feel comfortable with your presence.

On to to Deepeners and Ethics and whatever else crosses my mind while I am

going threw this, I am going to put in a few Deepeners that you can work with

and make your own, But these should serve as an example of what you are

looking for.

As a Hypnotherapist it's not always easy to know which sort of deepener to use with your clients - after all there are so many to choose from.

Does it Really Matter?

Well yes it does, This will take you back to your client questionnaire and your pre talk you had with them to find out what kinds of things relax them and so on.

I do not use scripts but when you are first starting out you need to use scripts as an example to give you a general idea of what to do , and what you are looking for and as soon as you a little experience you will want to start writing your own

script and then after a while you will be able to work without a script, Do not push yourself to try and get to this point, But it can be a problem trying to remember someone else's script but always remember that (what) hypnosis is not fragile and if you do mess up you can recover from a mistake and it should make no difference at all in the long run run, But you must just continue and act like nothing happened, Do not panic about the small thing, It is the overall results that you are looking for how you get to those results is not that important.

Just do your best be calm and do what you need to do. Before you are able to read this book I am going to post a lot of very helpful stuff on my web site so feel free to check it out for help when you need it and it will also keep you able to get in touch with me anytime you want to (http://Georgia-Hypnosis.webs.com) .

Deepening by Realization

In many instances of a subject.s first-time induction, the subject may not believe they are hypnotized. The use of the level one eye-stuck test serves as a convincer for them, realizing to their surprise that they cannot open their eyes. Upon encouraging them that they're doing well, you can then add .now relax and go

deeper.. You can achieve the same effect when a subject realizes that they cannot lower their arm in the level two test, or lose tract of their numbers in the level three test.

Pyramiding of Suggestions

Combine the utilization of pyramiding with the subjects realization they are, in

fact, experiencing hypnosis by suggestions such as, .On the count of three, your arm will go completely limp and fall loosely at your side.. The experiencing of this just after having the experience of having their arm made stiff and rigid, will serve to impress them even more, convincing them further that they are becoming hypnotized. Impressing the client with another surprise right after the realization that .something is happening,. will serve to deepen them. However, it's important.

That you don't use a demonstration that reaches beyond their immediate depth of trance. You want to be sure that you stop just short of failure. Otherwise you will have the effect of proving they are not as deep as you would like.

Post-hypnotic Suggestion

A simple and frequently used method is to give the subject a suggestion telling them, just before awakening, that the next time you hypnotize them, they will enjoy it more, go deeper more quickly and more easily.

This suggestion can be effective when you are re-hypnotizing the subject the same day, next day, several days later, or even a week later. It is helpful to integrate this suggestion, or a similar one, into every awakening as a matter of routine.

Repeated Induction Continued re-hypnotizing of a subject is a reliable way of deepening trance.

The procedure of re-inducing hypnosis has the effect of compounding the depth of the previous induction. The progress of relaxation seems to come in tiers.

After each induction the subject seems to respond to your suggestions from a more deeply relaxed state causing them to experience a deeper level of trance than in the previous induction.

Stage hypnotists use this phenomenon as part of their act. Each time they re hypnotize their subjects they then go on to more difficult tasks and demonstrations. Most subjects are extremely suggestible and VERY easy to hypnotize again for about ten minutes directly after awakening.

Counting Backwards

Counting backwards is a simple and reliable method of deepening. It can be done in different ways

Tell the client you will now count backwards from one hundred. On each count they will go deeper and deeper into hypnosis until at the count of one they will be as deep in hypnosis as they can go at this time.

A variation of the above counting method is to say the word .deeper. After each number.

Have the client count backwards and say the word .deeper. after each word while you begin talking. You can be giving them relaxing suggestions or another induction while they're counting which adds an element of confusion

Feedback Method

During the pre-talk, ask the client to describe their favorite place. Then, as they are hypnotized, feed back to them in details that appeal to all their senses, a vivid description of all the pleasures they would experience while at that place.

This takes skill that one can develop with some practice.

This Is A Script That Really Does Not Need A Deepener, But the reason I am posting in here right now is I have just found it and this can also be used for self hypnosis for confidence I use these still with self hypnosis, They will help you get ahead of the game and stay there, So more deepeners now.

Hypnosis For Confidence These suggestions and instructions are now going into your subconscious mind and they're having a greater influence over you... Every day these suggestions are becoming more effective and they are helping you in many different ways: spiritually, emotionally, physically, and mentally because every day in every way you are getting better and better.

Therefore, every suggestion that I am giving to your subconscious mind is already having a greater and greater influence over the way you think... Over the way you feel... And over the way you behave.

Even after you complete this brief session with me... After you have left here...

And you're no longer with me... These suggestions will continue influencing you just as strongly, just as surely... And Just as powerfully... As when you are with me here and now.

You have now become so deeply relaxed... So deeply relaxed and your mind has become so sensitive... So receptive to what I say... That everything that I put into your mind...

Will sink so deeply into the subconscious part of your mind... And will make so deep and lasting an impression there... That nothing will erase it.

In this condition, your subconscious mind is now at the

forefront; it is now readily accessible to my suggestions to you.

Each time I hypnotize you it keeps becoming more enjoyable... You relax to a deeper level... More peacefully... And with greater benefit. You will awaken more calm and relaxed... And will remain that way from today forward.

Your subconscious mind has already begun learning how quickly and easily you can calm yourself. This new knowledge allows your mind to be more clear, more alert, feel more refreshed, yet be more relaxed and more composed.

Consequently... These things that I've put into your subconscious mind... Will begin exercising greater and greater influence over the way you think... Over the way you feel... Over the way you behave.

And... Because these things will remain... Firmly embedded in the subconscious part of your mind... After you have left here... When you're no longer with me...

They will continue to exercise that same great influence... Over your thoughts... Your feelings... And your actions... Just as strongly... Just as surely, just as powerfully... When your back home or work.... As When your with me in this room.

You continue developing a more relaxed attitude, and you keep achieving more outstanding accomplishments in your life... Because everyday in every way you're getting better and better.

As a result of this deep hypnotic rest... You're going to feel physically stronger and fitter in every way. You will feel more alert... More wide awake... More energetic.

You will become much less easily tired... Much less easily fatigued...

Much less easily discouraged... Much less easily depressed. Every day... You will become so deeply interested in whatever you are doing... that your mind will become completely distracted away from yourself... you will no longer think nearly so much about yourself... You will no longer dwell nearly so much upon yourself and your difficulties... And you will become much less conscious of yourself... Much less preoccupied with yourself... And with your own feelings...

every day your nerves will become stronger and steadier... Your mind clearer...

More composed... More placid... More tranquil. You will become much less easily worried... Much less easily agitated... Much less fearful and apprehensive...

Much less easily upset.

As of tonight you'll be pleased to find that when you desire to sleep you'll sleep more deeply and more restfully than you have in the past. Your subconscious mind will work on solving any challenges that lie before you without disturbing your deep nurturing sleep.

In fact when you awaken totally refreshed, you will feel that the best description of your sleep was that it felt delicious.

Every day you will become aware that you are emotionally calmer... more settled... More stable... And able to function in all your activities in a relaxed confident way.

You are rapidly becoming all that you want to be: self confident...

Self-sufficient... Healthy... Acceptable... Capable... Admirable... And strong.

Your mind is powerful... It has brought you through the history of your past and all that has happened to you... And you realize that this is exactly what makes you unique and special.

The fact that you are making this effort right now to improve yourself shows you're open mindedness and searching nature are working in a creative way to improve yourself and grow.

You are now ready to live and let live... Feeling responsible for yourself and your feelings and choosing to let go of any old tapes created by someone else's opinion or attitude that has not served your purpose or goals.

All that you have done in your past has been either a successful accomplishment or a successful lesson.

Your past has all been a series of accomplishments or losses. These accomplishments and lessons have created a unique person you are today.

There is no one else on this earth exactly like you. You're confident in your uniqueness and secure in your accumulated wisdom... Wisdom that you have earned entitlement to You have learned and practiced acceptance whenever necessary and intuitively know when to push forward for a result you desire.

You recognize your right to choose your actions and your lifestyle and plan your activities, your goals, and your life based on your personal choices and desires.

You're confident in your life being what you choose and not someone else's opinion of You have outstanding capability... You have truly outstanding potential... You have the mental and physical ability to be an outstanding success... You'll keep developing more confidence in yourself each day... You willalways remember that success is a decision not good fortune. You are becoming successful because every day in every way you are getting better and better.

You already possess the ability to do everything you want to do... As well as everything you need to do... You have the talents, the skills, and the abilities.

For this reason you have complete and total confidence in yourself.

You have the ability to set good goals for yourself... And you have the determination, the confidence, and the motivation to consistently perform the actions necessary to achieve your goals-no matter what anyone else says.

You hereby claim your right... You affirm your freedom. Today you choose... With the greatest confidence... The way you will design the rest of your life.

You are experienced, intelligent, and have accumulated wisdom. Your entire past has been preparation for today... And today's the day... Your day... And to step forward in the realization to the deepest levels of your knowledge... That today truly is your day as you recognize how truly special you are.

This is the truth and the truth does not change.

Every day, in every way, you're getting better and better.

In a moment, I will count from one to five, and on the count of five you will open your eyes refreshed, alert, and eager to completely experience your fresh new outlook on life.

One, begin to allow your awareness to come back into this place.

Two, allow the energy to begin returning to your body beginning at your feet, moving up your legs.

Three, feel the energy now moving up throughout torso, wonderful revitalizing energy. Four, allow the energy to now move up into your shoulders and neck.

Five, and now the energy moves up into your head refreshing your mind, eyes open, wide awake, alert, and feeling wonderful.

DONE NOW YOU CAN ALSO CONVERT THIS TO SELF HYPNOSIS

Accelerated Learning Hypnosis Script - A special Learning Place

I found this script here, I am not usually impressed enough with a script to copy it but this ons not only is good, It is also a unique Idea and I wanted you all to have it, I feel that it may help you in your learning quest.

Script was written and placed on a page to be given away free by:

Alternative Practitioner Academy

- The Leidecker Institute -

This is a great script that I ran across and I will

A Special Learning Place

This procedure has been used with incredible success in many applications. I

developed it for a person going to college thirty- six years after high school graduation.

She received A's and A pluses in every test even though she never did nearly that well in high school.

You are welcome to use and copy this script freely. It is copyrighted only to prevent anyone else from copyrighting it and preventing me from using my own material.

It has been successful for attorneys taking their bar exams and doctors taking their medical exams.

It is very important that you read this script slowly.

Use an appropriate induction method. Be sure during the induction the subject is

using their thumb and index finger together as a triggering device which will also be used later for recall.

As you read, it is important to allow your subject sufficient time to process each instruction. It will be especially helpful if your subject knows self hypnosis. Now I would like you to visualize or imagine yourself looking at your brain . . . Imagine that you can see it right in front of you, close enough that if you were to reach out, you could touch it. Imagine now that you are enlarging the image of it . . . . Now imagine that you're looking inside of it.

What you're looking for is a place that you can use for a special learning purpose and for storing information.

I don't know whether you will find this place in your right hemisphere or your left hemisphere . . . It doesn't really matter much which hemisphere you use because either side will work very well for increasing your learning capacity.

I would like you to look for this place from inside your brain . . .

Good.

This place can be a part of your brain that you've never used before or it can be a part that you haven't needed to use much lately . . . When you've found it your right index finger will lift upwards.

I'd like for you to take a moment and prepare this place for new activity .

. . You may have to clean it out, or you may have to just brighten it up a little to get it ready to start actively serving you . . . I'll be quiet a moment while you do that . . . Now I'd like you to take a moment and ask your subconscious mind to show your conscious mind where this place is.

After you've shown your conscious mind where this place is, your right index finger will lift up.

Good.

Now have your subconscious mind show your conscious mind how to

open this special place . .

Good.

Now ask your subconscious mind to show your conscious mind how to file or put information into this special place. You can store information you read, hear in lectures, see in videos, or study with audio cassettes.

You can either use a file cabinet or a computer or any other way you choose to put this information into your special place . . . I'll be quiet a moment while you have your subconscious mind show your conscious mind how to put information in your special place.

When you've finished, your right index finger will lift upwards.

Good.

Now have your subconscious mind show your conscious mind how to close your special place so that whatever information you put or file in there will be there for you when you want it . . Have your conscious mind close that place once just to see that it knows how.

Good.

You have now located and prepared a special place to store everything you wish to retain . . . You have shown your conscious mind how to open this place . . . How to put information into this place . . . And how to close

this place . . .

From today forward, whenever you begin to study or listen to a lecture, you will first roll up your eyes, take a deep breath, slowly close your eyelids while still keeping your eyes up, then exhale, relax your eyes, float down and touch your thumb and finger together, and visualize opening your storage place to receive the information.

Then when you've opened your storage place, open your eyes and begin studying.

Upon finishing your studying, close the place the same way . . . If you need to, you can roll your eyes up secretly by holding your hand to your forehead for a moment, covering your eyes.

Each time you need your stored information, or when taking a test, you will first roll up your eyes, take a deep breath, slowly close your eyelids while still keeping your eyes up, then exhale, relax your eyes, float down and touch your thumb and finger together, and visualize opening your storage place and mentally visualizing yourself retrieving the needed information from your files, computer, or whatever method you have created.

Should you not immediately be able to locate the information

needed, go ahead with your test or whatever you're doing knowing the answer will just "pop" into your head in a very short time.

Now count out your subject in your usual manner.

One more I just had to put in here for you guys and this one is also compliments of:

Alternative Practitioner Academy

- The Leidecker Institute -

Sexual Enhancement.

Your guess is as good as mine so lets find out together what do you say.

Sex Enhancement Script

This script is offered for enhancing sexual experiences. It is not intended

as an alternative to professional therapy.

Roll your eyes up, all the way up as if you're looking at your hairline through your forehead. Take a big deep breath and hold it . Slowly close just your eyelids. . .

Now exhale, relax, and float down.

Take another deep breath and as you exhale, allow your relaxation to flow down and throughout your body.

As you continue breathing, comfortably, allow yourself to relax more and more each time you exhale.

Start Music

Induction

(Include instructions to let any noises fade into the background as

necessary.)

Allow this time that we spend together now to be a gift of relaxation to yourself.

Any thoughts or things you need to do can be just set aside for these few moments.

They will be there for you when we're finished.

So just relax. Just for a moment, imagine all the muscle groups in your body relaxing and letting go . . . as all the sensory receptors in your body begin to open and revitalize.

Each time that you breathe from this time forward, imagine your breath flowing out through your rib cage and spreading sensual relaxation throughout your

body . . . So feel that relaxation as I talk to you now.

Lets start by relaxing all the muscle groups around your face for a moment . . .

Relax your scalp . . . relax your forehead . . . relax your eyebrows . . . relax your

eyelids . . . relax your cheeks . . . relax your nose . . . and relax your mouth.

Especially those muscles around your mouth and lips. Become especially aware of

your sense of feeling around your mouth and lips.

Make sure your teeth are not clenched together . . . Just relax your chin and jaw .

. . And allow all those muscles in your face to just relax and let go . . . And now

relax your neck . . . relax the front part of your neck, and the back part of your

neck.

Right down through to your shoulders . . . Feel your shoulders relaxing

completely as you let go of any tension that might be lingering in your shoulder

area . . . You'll find it feels so good to do that.

Allow your arms to relax now . . . Relax your upper arms . . . relax your elbows . .

. relax your forearms, relax your wrists . . . your hands. Even your fingers relax

and let go . . . as they become more pleasantly sensitive to every touch and

feeling . . . Just imagine your arms becoming very heavy, loose, and limp.

Heavy . . . loose . . . and comfortable.

Allow yourself to breathe comfortably now . . . and notice how smooth and even

your breathing has become compared to just a few moments ago when we

started.

Feel your breathing . . . Feel the nice sensual rhythm of your breathing . . . Notice

the contraction and expansion of your diaphragm and your chest as you allow

your chest muscles to relax completely . . . Right down through to your stomach.

Feel your stomach muscles just relaxing as you let go of any stress or tension

that might be lingering in that area . . . Now allow your back muscles to relax . . .

The large muscles in the upper part of your back, right down your spinal column

and into your lower back . . . Just letting go . . . Letting go completely. And allow

those smaller muscle groups in the lower part of your back to relax as well.

Now your hips relax . . . and allow an increased stimulating flow of blood to enter

your lower abdomen and thigh area. . . relax your thighs . . . relax your

knees . . . relax your calves . . . relax your ankles . . . relax your feet, and even

relax your toes . . . Just allow those muscle groups to relax completely as you

begin to drift, to drift into a very deep, relaxed state. Letting yourself go . . .

Letting your mind and body become one . . . Feeling good . . . Feeling so much

better than before . . . . Some people relaxing there as you are experience certain

stimulating feelings in their body.

Some people experience a tingling feeling in their arms, legs, and inner thighs

(such as tiny, painless pins and needles). Some people experience a warmness in

their body yet others experience energy . . . If you're experiencing warmth or

sensual energy, go with that feeling. Relax and allow those feelings to flow throughout your body.

The important thing that this level of relaxation represents, is that if you're

experiencing any of these sensations, its an indication of your willingness and

readiness to go into hypnosis and allow any unwanted inhibitions to simply float

away . . . float away . . . Going into hypnosis can be very gradual and in a

moment I'm going to count from twenty to one.

On each count you can allow yourself to drift . . .to drift into hypnosis at your

own pace.

But before I begin counting, just imagine a custom cloud snuggling up to your

body in the shape of a chair . . . And imagine this chair has arms on it. It is a

very warm and comfortable cloud . . . Its your personal cloud . . . Feel how it

snuggles up to your body Allow this cloud to take you to a very, very beautiful,

sensual, and romantic place . . . A special place in your life . . . Maybe a place in

your memory . . . Maybe a place you imagine as being ideal. A very comfortable

place . . . A place where you're happy. A place where you're in perfect shape and

health . . . A place where you look good . . . So allow this custom cloud now to

just snuggle up to your body and to take you to your special place . . . where

you're happy, relaxed, and feeling very sensual. Just allow yourself to be there for

a moment and soon I'll begin to count and you can take yourself deeper and

deeper into hypnosis and the awareness that your sense of taste, touch, and

smell has been keenly awakened.

20, . . . Just letting go now . . . 19, . . . all the way down deep . . . 18, . . .feeling

better than before . . . 17, . . . tired and drowsy . . . 16, . . . peaceful and

serene . . .15, . . . awakening your sexual being . . . 14, . . . arousing all your

senses . . . 13, . . . arousing every fiber, . . . 12, . . . arousing every cell . . . 11,

deeper and deeper . . . 10, . . . happy and letting go now . . . 9, . . . confident

and secure . . . 8, 7 . . . enjoying the relaxation . . . 6, 5 . . . just letting go now .

. . 4, 3 . . . deeper and deeper . . . 2, . . . And finally, 1 . . . deep, deep, deep

hypnosis.

Your mind is now very relaxed and open to receive the helpful and beneficial suggestions I'm about to give you.

(Add your additional suggestions that are appropriate to your clients goals here.)

In a moment I'll count to the number five and you'll awaken refreshed, alert and

feeling wonderful in every way. You'll be amazed at the wonderful difference that

this brief session of hypnosis has created for you.

Bringing your awareness back into this room now.

Allowing the energy to begin rising in your body, starting at your feet and moving

up your legs.

Wonderful energy moving up throughout your torso now.

Bring that energy up through your neck and shoulders now.

And now that wonderful energy moves up into your head making your mind

fresh, clear, alert. Open your eyes now, wide awake, alert, and feeling great.

Alright now that was a wonderful script, And I would like for you to look back over

it because it has a lot of information in one script, It shows the proper way to do deepener, This script is an ideal script to base your idea of what a script should on, This script has ever thing, Well except an awakener, we are going to talk about the importance of awakener right about now, Ans as I run into things I feel

will be of interest to all of you I will still stop and post them along the way, This was a must post because it is the example of an almost perfect script so please pay close attention to what they did all through that script and I will move along now.

Norman Bowman C.Ht

CHAPTER 10
AWAKENER'S AN A LOT OF OTHER STUFF

By now I am sure that you have noticed what chapter I am in or what I am discussing really means nothing to me when I have a thought of something I feel you would like to know or need to know I go ahead and write it in anyway I am sorry about that, But if I feel that I have found something or have remembered something that may help you along the way I write it in anywhere I am at, Itkeeps me from having to go back and change everything in the whole book.

I would like to think that you appreciate me thinks of your well being by doing this but I know many of you think it is a pain in the rear end, So I am taking this opportunity to say I am sorry for that, But I am going to keep doing it so lets get to some awakener's.

I want to say before I begin to show you these that this is very important even if you do not think you got the person in a trance because there is no way to be sure weather you did or did not, So there fore you cannot take a chance you must go through the awakener's every time, EVERY TIME because you cannot be sure and a person could go out and get hit by a bus or have a car wreck because you did not take time to properly awaken them, I hope I have made myself clear on how important it is to do this and it really only takes a couple of minutes to be absolutely sure, So please do this every time.

Awakener's are easy but they must be done, Although a person can't become stuck in a hypnotic state, it's highly important to help him make the transition slowly and comfortably instead of having him jarred back into reality, which could be traumatic and do damage to the work you've accomplished in your session.

Counting slowly and methodically backward is a simple way to help your patient re-emerge.

Tell the clients that it's now time to leave the state he has been in. Say something like, "I am now going to count backward from five to one. With each number, you

will feel more alert and present in the room. With each number I say, you will become more aware of your senses."

Count backward beginning with five. Between the numbers, have the client focus on one specific thing to do. You can say things like, "Four. You are now aware of your hands and feet. Three. You are more alert. Two. You are re-emerging. And one, your eyes are open and you are present in the room."

Now ask the person to speak and tell you how she feels.

Alright we have covered a lot of ground so far in this book, This is probably one of the most important things we have covered so far because it is very important to your client, I am going to post the hypnotist ethics now and we will talk about them a bit and I am going to move back to self hypnosis for the remainder of the book unless something else comes to mind, So lets do it.

At this time we are going to move on to guess what a lot of other stuff, There are many things in this book that I have not explained as well as I should have, Know this though if you have read this book you have contact information to get in touch with me and I will always be there to help you anyway I can to get where you want to get to in life.

Now I am basically just going to ramble on a little more about everything and once in a while I hope some useful information comes out of my ramblings, So let do it. I want to talk some more about self hypnosis and the benefits it gives you in all aspects of your life, It simply breaks down to the FACT that if you think you

are a winner you are a winner. And self hypnosis and mediation can give you a winners mindset, I want all of you to have this winning mindset, So I am going to break down and write you some affirmation's that I will tell you how to use everyday and I expect you to use them, (Because You Are All Winners) so it is time the rest of the world knows it.

After I give you these affirmations I will show you step by step how to use them in your everyday life and then we are going to work on positive speech patterns that are also worth there weight in gold. (Before I am done you will recommend this book to all of your friends and family) I just know it , lol .

You must develop a habit of using positive affirmations constantly, It is important to you because the more you use them the more you will believe them and the more people you deal with daily will believe them, Now you may be thinking that if I start doing this everyone will think I am nuts, So what.

What is more important to you living a full happy life where you can give your family everything they need or to be thought crazy, Myself I would rather be thought crazy and be wonderfully happy, Than to be what everyone thinks I should be and live a miserable life with no hopes of it ever improving.

Here are a few to get you started while I think about more.

This is important, if you think back I some what covered this before it is very very important that you be grateful for what you already have, Before you will be trusted with more, I prosper wherever I turn and I know that I deserve prosperity of all kinds The more grateful I am, the more reasons I find to be grateful.

Alright lets be real here no one pays there bills with love, But when you pay

your bills know that you always have more money coming so it does not matter, Just pay them with a smile on your face because you know something not everyone knows and that is that God will never let your wallet get empty, Yes it may get empty, But you KNOW in your heart that it will never stay that way. I want you to be grateful of everything you have, Think about it, Everyone has things to be grateful for, Yes we all do and if you can not see them then close this book throw it in the trash because I will never be able to help you.

When I think God for the things in my life I thank him for every breath I take and every beat of my heart, I thank him for loving me because he loves us all, I thank him for my home and my car, I thank him for the fact that I am not driving uninsured, I thank him for the fact that I have been able to do remolding on my home, Don t sit around and dwell on the fact that your home needs work be thankful that you were able to fix the faucet or whatever, Be positive, Without gratitude you will never be given anything else.

Put yourself in the place of a child, If you have kids think about the time you bought your child a toy and he destroyed it in the first ten second after he received it, Then ran up and wanted to go to the store and pick out another,

What did you tell him, If you had any sense anyway, When you learn to appreciate what you have I will give you some more.

Well what makes you think you are exempt from the same kind of rough justice, Well you are not, And when you start to appreciate what you have then and only then will you be given more, That is a fact live with it, Now I also know that there are a few people out there that will never be able to be thankful for what they have, And they will never have more.

They are bitter mean people who want to go through life with a ton of things to whine and cry about, As a matter of fact they get off on the whining they do not want more because they would never have anything to talk about, If there life was full and happy they would be miserable because that is the kind of person they are.

They must spend there time feeling sorry for themselves for fear no one else will, At least that is what I believe, Don't be like them find things to thank God for everyday, Tell other people how wonderful life is and how truly blessed you are and God will rain down abundance on your life like you would have never believed possible.

Oh and by the way I believe in God, But that is not the point either, Weather or not you believe in God or not, the same participles still apply, The cosmic forces or karma or whatever you wish to label things still work on the same principles you must appreciate what you have before life or karma or whatever will entrust you with more, That my friends is FACT.

So positive affirmations really just keep positive things going through your mind while you develop a positive attitude yourself, So what are we dealing with here, We are dealing with another form of self hypnosis, Although, I feel all forms are needed to get to where you need to be in life.

Being pitiful is a way of life, Being bitter and mean are a way of life, So we all need to make every effort possible not too be this way, Alright positive affirmation, I am going to try and give you a few more before I go off on my next tangent, All of the affirmations I am about to give you are true and there is not much that I can say about them so here we go.

I know that I deserve Love and accept it now

• I give out Love and it is returned to me multiplied

• I rejoice in the Love I encounter everyday

These are good true affirmations, I cannot find anything here to have a fit

about so lets move on quickly. To the next affirmations.

I have a wonderful partner and we are both happy and at peace

• I release any desperation and allow love to find me

• I attract only healthy relationships

OK once again I think these are great affirmations so lets move on to the

next ones.

I am the perfect weight for me

• I choose to make positive healthy choices for myself

• I choose to exercise regularly

When I believe in myself, so do others

• I express my needs and feelings

• I am my own unique self - special, creative and wonderful

The last affirmations were quite good I thought, So a few more.

All my relationships are loving and harmonious

• I am at peace

• I trust in the process of life

Life is a joy filled with delightful surprises

• My life is a joy filled with love, fun and friendship all I need do is

stop all criticism, forgive, relax and be open.

• I choose love, joy and freedom, open my heart and allow

wonderful things to flow into my life.

These are great affirmations and I suggest you use them as often as

possible,

I am going to stop right here and tell you a little about myself and why the

information I am giving you is good, It works, It can change your life for the

better and that is what I want for all of you, So lets here about me.

First I never did anything in my life other than construction, I was an

industrial electrician, Most of my life and that took me to 48 states and 5, 3rd world countries.

I was a some what functioning Drug Addict form the time I was 13 years old until I was 28, Then I quit using Drugs and turned into an instant alcoholic and that is the way I lived my life, I worked I drank and I lost.

Being highly skilled at what I did always left me in a situation where I could always get a job, Otherwise I would have been homeless and helpless, When I was 40 I screwed my back up very bad and I could not continue to do what I had been doing my whole life and I was left with a lot of time on my hands,

I got interested in hypnosis and physiology as a way to control my own pain, Not because I was above just taking pain pills for the pain but because the pain pills would not control my pain it was so bad, As a matter of fact before my first surgery I was plotting my own death because the pain was more that I could bear, So I started looking at physiology and hypnosis as a means to control my own pain.

I have always been good at every type work I have done including what I am doing now but I was never good at anything else, I could never get along with anyone for more than awhile and always when I got tired of anything I just left, Let me change that when things got difficult I ran away that is more the truth of the situation, I was never able to hold onto a relationship.

I was never any good to my family including a child that I owe a lot to, Anyway before this starts to look like I am whining I am going to move onto why my information is good it is because these methods no matter how bad my writing is these methods have completely changed my life and the life of others around me.

Now I am happy and well adjusted, I am a very good hypnotist, But that's not the important part now I know how to live and be happy, Now I can have relationships, Now I have something to offer the people I am around and it is for the most part due to Gods loving grace that has made it all possible but I had to change a lot about my life before God started to work in my life and the things I have written in this book are how I made the changes so no matter what you think these methods do work and they just may save your life so why don't you let them, Start practicing the things in this book as best you can and let the magic that they can bring on just happen in your life.

It does not happen in a few minutes but it happens much faster than you think, And if your life is in a mess like mine was you really have nothing to lose. The first and foremost thing you have to do is to forgive, You also have to realize that what others do is not because they are bad people it is because they are suffering from a condition, And the condition they suffer from is being human, So now when someone does something that I do not agree with or that makes me mad instead of thinking how terrible they are for doing it I just think well that is just a very human thing to do.

We must give up hatred because it does not hurt the ones we hate it tears us apart from the inside out, And it makes it impossible for us to ever be happy.

The next thing is guilt, The hardest I think, I still suffer with it and believe me I have really been a terrible person, REALLY, And you have to realize that God is bigger than anything human, And that we are not able to comprehend what God can forgive, Then we have to come around to believing he has forgiven us and start trying to forgive ourselves and I will tell you it is just about impossible to do, But I have finally forgiven myself.

And without that I could have never been where I am in life right now.

Compassion, Do you have that I mean really, Are the needs of others more important than your own, I always felt sorry for people at least I had that going for me but do you really care, If you really cared you would do everything you possible could do to relive the suffering of others, No I do not mean you must join the peace corp or something you make things right in your life, What I mean is just try to do the things in your own control to never ever add to someones pain and suffering and when you can do something to make it better.

Life is a gift, And it really is what we make of it, Once you start caring about others and doing the things you can to make there lives better then a wealth of good fortune will fall onto of you that you will not ever be able to dig out of.

Yes you will be just covered up good things, And you will also be happy, See all good things really do come from within, Bill Gates is one of the most successful people on earth and I know nothing of him personally, But what I know about Bill Gates tells me that he is probably one of the best ever software geniuses of all times, I was a very high paid electrician and what that said about me is I was a good electrician but no matter how much money I made I had to borrow money on Wednesday to get me through till payday.

So I was a good electrician but a poor person.

With what I know now I would have much rather been a bad electrician and a good person, When you do good for others it is not about going out and telling everyone you did it because that says that you want others to do even better things for you because you had a kind moment, What if you do something nice and keep it to yourself, Well that is much better because you know you did all you could do and expected nothing more than to help a person, And the healing inside you begins, Every good things this life has to offer comes from the inside and works its way out, Once you begin to act you feel better about yourself, I am at a point I can seem to think of anything else to say can you believe it.

Once you begin the healing process on the inside the things on the outside will start to heal also, When you begin to be happy you begin to smile and when you begin to smile you invite others into your life, And one thing leads to another, success is not measured by how good of a hypnotist you are but as to how good of a person you are, So trust me when I say all good things come from within, Start to change what is on the inside and you will find everything else will fall into place in record time.

Allow your self to be happy, Do nice things for others, And no your are not that bad a person and invite good things into your life by wearing a smile, You can walk with a spring in your step because you are a good and caring person, I placed some information on covert hypnosis and Nlp in this book, I suggest that you use them to help others any time you get a chance, Use the Anchors to make others happy it is very simple, Remember how I told you to use the anchors like (You Are Always Happy) Right.

The anchor is you are always happy, And the right is the part that keeps you from looking like a fool, Use the stop smoking anchors often and on everyone you can as I said they do not work on everyone but they do work on some and if you can help one person stop smoking you may have added years to his or hers life so use it even if they do think you are nuts it is worth it, It is also leaving a person knowing that you left them with a suggestion to always be happy, Hypnosis is one of the closest things to magic that we all have at our disposal so use it to help everyone you meet and you will find that you are a happier person.

Do not let the fact that hypnosis did not work on one person stop you from using it on others because it works more than it fails, I am going to tell you a little secret, When I was in my 20's I got into a little trouble with the law and the judge ordered me to see a psychiatrist, So I did in order to stay out of jail, But here is the funny part, He ended up wanting to hypnotize me and I did not believe that I could be hypnotized and there fore I could not be hypnotized, If you run into someone who says that they cannot be hypnotized, Move on they are not worth your time, But the secret is that if I wanted to spend the time on them there is no one on earth that I cannot hypnotize and that is a fact.

If a person refuses your help move on unless you have a personal vestment in that person, Because it is a huge waste of time, I have honed my skill to where I am hypnotizing everyone I meet from the moment I meet them till the moment I leave them by everything I do and everything I do, You can also do this, It just takes time, But first you have to understand how hypnosis works and I feel that I told you that as well as I could, You must now meditate and I don't mean meditate like go into a deep meditation I mean it as in give what I told you a lot of thought and think of ways to do what I told you needed to be done.

I told you that hypnosis is talking directly with the subconscious, And to be able to do this we have to trick our way past the conscious mind, There are millions of ways to do this, You just need to take the information you have and find ways to use it, I am doing another book on just covert suggestions if you wish to get one of these books just go to my web site send me an email and ask for the book, I intend to do a lot of your thinking for you, But remember sometimes it is better just to wing it rather than waste your time trying to remember word for word what someone else has said.

I never write anything that I expect you to remember word for word anyway everything I write down here for you is to be used as an example only, But the book I am telling you is coming soon will be loaded with things I have done and they worked for me and they will without a doubt work for you.

Do not let anyone on any web site or in any book tell you that things have to be done exactly the way they have done them, That is just not true, It is the hypnosis that does the work not the hypnotist, I have read things that others have wrote where they call them self a hypnosis guide, this is closer to the truth and I am not sure at all that that is the proper way to say it, Well

I am your guide right now and we are going to make the best of our time together by me telling you there is no such thing as perfect hypnosis and it will work almost every time if you use the proper principles.

Other peoples methods do not work for me I use what I learn from another person as a general pattern or idea and then I do it my way or the way it happens when I do it, I am impressed by many hypnotist and the way they seem just to hypnotize people with so little effort, But remember that is them that is what works good for them you are another person with a whole different personality and you are comfortable with different things than they are so what works for them may well not work for you, That is another reason I feel that people give up on learning hypnosis is they try it and it does not work and they think well I did everything just exactly the same way he did and it did not work so I guess I am just not cut out for this, WRONG, you can be as good as him or maybe even better.

The first thing you need to do is to quit trying to do it just like he did it, That is your first problem is trying to do it his way you need to do the same thing but you need to do it your way not his, Everything on every web site you look at and in any book you read should be looked at as general information on a subject, You should never try and duplicate what another person does exactly because the sames things do not work for all people, Another thing is you would not attempt to hypnotize a person that is in a bar the same way you would hypnotize a person in a mall, And you would never use the same techniques that worked in a bar in your office.

Earlier in the book I was tooting Derren Browns horn and bragging on some of the things he does well he is one of the best there is but Derren does things how they work best for Derren and if you were to attempt to copy him chances are that it would not work for you. I am very much a fan of Derren but I do not know him and probably never will but what I get from his vid's is that he is a very high energy fast talking type of hypnotist that I could never copy in real life, But that does not mean that I can not duplicate the things he does by doing them my way.

What I am saying is that you will develop your own style of doing this and I am sure when you do, That you will be able to do anything that any other hypnotist does just as well as they can but you will do them your way and I bet no one will be able to copy you either so there you go, I am very good at what I do, And I read and tried other people methods and some of them even worked for me but then I finally understood that I would be much better off if I started to put my own twist on things, Things that work for other people do not work for me and as I said somewhere in the book earlier, I am a kind of intimidating person. It is not something I do on purpose but I told you a little about my life and when you are working in certain places or a certain kind of people you must carry yourself in a way that would make them think several times before messing with you and I have that persona I don't mean to I just have it from being in those situations for so many years, I try to smile and give people a since of well being around me but it still needs more work, And that is something else I am working on.

Alright take writing these books for instance, I am not a writer, I know I am not good at this but what I am hoping for is that the message that I am putting out there in my books will get people to look over my skill as writer and look at the message at least until I get better at it and I have faith that it is going to be like that, And by the way I am working on learning to write,

But the message I am putting out needs to be out there people need this message so I am willing to take a chance on what people think of me to get the message out there, remember when I said earlier about what people think of you really does not matter and if your message is pure they will come around to believing in you sooner or later and that is a fact.

I have faith in God and I have faith in people that I will do just fine despite my lack of skill in writing because the message I am writing about is much more important than the writing itself, Do not ever let another person trample your dream, Some people get joy out of hurting others, But good people are the majority and the majority rules now and forever, I will count on the good people in the world to get my message out, We're all one anyway, We are a team we cannot be broken up by the bad people in the world we will stick together and overcome all obstacle's and that is what I am trying to show you how to do, To the best of my ability.

I believe in everyone until shown otherwise (We Will All Stick Together) I want this book to get to as many people as possible because I think it will help everyone it reaches to have a much better life, Let us look at other ways we can help others with our new found skills, Obesity kills people everyday and you know you can help people not fall into the trap of being over weight by simply telling them something like.

Say something to this effect when you see someone eating unhealthy foods, Be careful with this one and do not under any circumstances say it with sarcasm, If they eat to much junk food you can help them by saying, Or at least I hope this goes well for you, It must be wonderful to be able to splurge and eat something like that, It is because (You Always Eat Healthy)

I am not sure how to pull this one off but you should work on it and find a comment that works in the situation you are in, Be careful, lol Let me move on to another Anchor before I get you killed, Om lets try it this another way, (You Love To Exercise) that is your anchor and the saver is once again RIGHT, Plant this on a person that you feel would be better off exercising a tad more, The saver the word right may not only save you from looking like your crazy with some of these anchors it just may save your life, lol , You van however make people want to exercise in this way, Another way to do this is to say something much safer like, You must (work out a lot) to stay as fit as you are, Work out a lot is your anchor and to stay as fit as you are.

 Is your saver, And you just may need saving when dealing with this subject, Lets move on.

Another is (You Are Just Happy) that is your anchor, Your saver is I can just see it in your face, This can help change a person from having a terrible day to have a great day quick like, Another is, (You Feel Great Today) Right,

Alright I am going to move on now and remember these are generalizations and you must figure out how to place them into conversations as well as you can, But remember you can control any situation or conversation in this manner, Not only that you can control how one person or a whole group of people feel about you like this, So what are you waiting on, Lets start right now.

I am going to move to ethics and as always if something I feel you cannot live without hearing comes up I stop and write it in.

Pretty Much The End Of This Book Please Look For The Next One

9 CHAPTER

HYPNOTIST ETHICS

Hypnosis is very powerful and valuable method of changing another person's perception, understanding, and fundamental mental processes. It can be used to alter the subject's reality. Because of the potential for abuse of such an **influential technique** the first step in learning to become a hypnotist is to adopt a personal code of ethics. Not only will this code provide guidelines for you as a hypnotist, it is also required of all students to agree to abide this code or they cannot learn hypnosis through our tutelage.

Plus mentioning you obey a strict code of ethics is a boon when offering to entrance the pub patron on the another bar stool.

The Hypnotist Code of Ethics

1. A hypnotist has a unique **bond of trust** with the hypnotic subject therefore a

hypnotist must always maintain a concern for their subject's welfare, respect their

personal rights and dignity, practice social responsibility, and maintain their own

professional integrity.

A hypnotist must always obtain **consent** of the subject before attempting to hypnotize them.

The **well being** of the subject must be the prime concern of the hypnotist.

A hypnotist must not attempt to **treat** medical disorders, unless they are a trained medical professional. Any subject with a medical problem must be urged to seek proper professional medical treatment.

A hypnotist must become familiar with, and **obey** all laws and regulations regarding the performance of hypnosis in the jurisdictions in which they practice.

Because of the unique relationship and **emotional rapport** between hypnotist and subject, a hypnotist specifically will not use hypnosis as an advantage to engage in business dealings or in relationships of a sexual nature with any subject.

A hypnotist will always make post hypnotic suggestions of **positive well being** to hypnotized subjects.

A hypnotist will never intentionally cause strong or frightening emotions, obscene or sexual hallucinations, or degrading suggestions without the prior non hypnotized

consent of the subject.

The End

I want to thank everyone who read this book despite my challenges as a writer and know I am working on being able to bring you many quality written books in the future, Also below are some ways to contact me with any problems that you may have, Also remember that I am willing to help you anyway I ca to become the hypnotist and the person you wish to be.

E-mail: Georgia.hypnosis@mail.com

We Site: Georgia-hypnosis.webs.com

Personal: Jhonst1234@ymail.com

I would also ask that if you enjoyed this book to please let me know, It will give me the incentive to write more of this type book or please let me know what you would have me write about.

Thank You

Norman Bowman C.Ht

Learn Hypnosis Use This Magic To Live A Happy

ABOUT THE AUTHOR

There is not a lot I can say about myself except that I am extremely blessed person to be where I am to day and there has been many people in my life that if it had not been for them I would have never made it to be here today, I would like to also like to say that God has been good to me in every way and if it were not for Gods kindness and the mercy he has shown to me I would not be here Thank You To everyone who reads this book, I am still in school and I will probably always find a reason to take another class, Education is priceless and if anyone anywhere anytime needs help finding a school please feel free to contact me I will help anyone I can.

I would also like to add that I was in my late 40's when I decided to continue my education so for those of you who think you are too old to go back to school I am living proof that it is never to late, I am at this moment taking writing classes that you can see I need badly, And I am continuing my education in Psychology which I am fascinated with.

Thank You Norman Bowman C.Ht C.Rc

www.ingramcontent.com/pod-product-compliance
Lightning Source LLC
Chambersburg PA
CBHW070536290526
45790CB00002B/517